The Life-Testimony and Work of a Servant of God

By:

Patricia A. Harrigan

Table of Contents

Preface

This is the author's very first book. Patricia A. Harrigan is a devout woman of God, who has lived her entire life in the House of God, involved in Christian service.

Converted to Christ in her early years at eleven, Patricia took great delight in developing herself in the Christian faith. Apart from her own willingness and determination to blossom as a child of God, she attributes much of her growth to her mother who was particularly careful to see her walking diligently in the straight and narrow after her conversion and baptism.

She also enjoyed the support of her siblings, especially her older brothers, who watched out for her wellbeing. But more importantly, in her spiritual walk she benefitted much from the pastors and elders of the church who watched out for her soul, even after she was matured in the faith.

Being seasoned in the faith through the grace of Christ, Patricia continued to grow spiritually as time went on. At the age of 23, she was married and made a home of her own. The Lord blessed her with three wonderful sons, Patmore, Patison and Patville, whom she was careful to nourish in the ways of God.

Still desirous of more of God, and eager to continue in His service, Pat dedicated her talents to become a gospel singer, was ordained as Minister of Worship, and Pastor. She was later ordained as Prophetess. Like the prophets of old, her works speak for her.

It is from this angle of Christian service that she decided to write this book. This book is not just about Patricia, but it's about the call of God on her life – a call that would touch and influence the lives of others. So, be inspired and encourage as you read.

Introduction

If I were to say why I wrote this book, the reason would be perfectly wrapped up in seven immortal words: "to tell of the goodness and greatness," of God.

I am sure that I speak for true Christians everywhere and Mankind in general, when I say that God has been good to us. If you are a Christian, it is no doubt that you, too, can rightfully attest to the fact that "God is good". By the way, he is not just "good", but I am sure you would agree that He is "great". His greatness and goodness are evident throughout the entire earth – throughout the farthest reaches of His great universe.

Therefore, I concur with the Psalmist David (of old times) who thought deeply of the goodness of God, and as he considered His awesome acts, he exclaimed: *"Great is the Lord, and greatly to be praised."* I agree too, with Jen Johnson, who, (in modern times) reflected on God's benevolent goodness and sang: *"For all my life He has been faithful, for all my life He has been so, so good."* What a great reflection of the goodness of God.

This book relates how the hand of God has rested upon my life from the moment that I yielded to His son, Jesus, who once said: *"Come unto me. All ye who are weary and heavy laden and I will give you rest."* I dare say that though I was not so much burdened by the heavy weight of sins as a child, when I came to Him, still as a young innocent girl of Saddlers, St. Kitts, an island in the Caribbean, I needed His rest. I needed the assurance of God's great salvation so full and free.

Consequently, this book describes the circumstances under which I yielded my life to Christ. It tells how I developed in the Lord from the youthful stage of a child, coming up in the ranks of church life. It relates how great an impact my hometown church has had upon my upbringing through the quality mentorship of my Pastors and Elders. The *support* and *pattern* of righteous living were laid out before me in such a way that I could not defy *them* and live as I please. No! In fact, I did not want to live any old how.

I was hungry and thirsty for the kind of fervor and dedication with which my mentors faithfully served the Lord. The characteristics of their pilgrimage and service mapped out for me a lifestyle of responsibility and accountability that I have grown to emulate. So indebted to them, and committed to the cause of Christ, I could not do otherwise.

"The Life-Testimony and Work of God's Servant" reflects an account of my spiritual development and devotion to the Lord, who had called me to live a life of light and purpose before Him. Very importantly, it shows how God uses a life that is surrendered to His divine will in order to reach out to others who are in need of healing, restoration and His divine protection.

I use this book to encourage other Christians to be determined to draw closer to God. There is no better place on earth to be than to be in His presence. If you, as a Christian would decide to draw close to Him, you will discover the bliss that He brings as He, in turn, draws close to you. So, allow your life to count for God's purpose. Allow your life to bask in His presence.

Though *"The Life-Testimony and Work of God's Servant"* tells of my life's experiences in Christ, still it is not intended to be all about me. It is for the purpose of helping you to substantiate your relationship with the Lord. As you read, I pray that the Holy Spirit would enlighten your mind, inspire you, and give you a desire to allow Him to influence your life. It is my sincere hope that like me, you too would be determined to continue your journey in God.

So, please savor the reading as the Holy Spirit directs your thoughts and enrich your life.

Chapter 1:

"My Born-Again Experience

and Faith in Christ"

My conversion and spiritual journey as a born again Christian, began in 1968 at tender age of eleven in my little home church, the Church of God of Prophecy, in Saddlers Village, St. Kitts, in the Caribbean. I am the third child, and first girl of a family of four girls and eight boys.

The year 1968 was a dreadful and solemn one for me. It was the year when Martin Luther King was assassinated. This sent shockwaves of global mourning throughout the world, and it seemed like all of earth's functions had ceased for a while. The very silence of household animals depicted the impact of such an ordeal. It was the untimely death of a stalwart of faith and promise – and a freedom fighter for the black race. The morbid circumstances that surrounded King's death produced a scary, solemn moment for me.

I recalled churches and Governments around the Caribbean – and the world at large – ushering in unified prayer services in respect of this great Leader who had spent his life advocating freedom for the oppressed black race all around the world. It was in that moment, so dismal and sad, that I felt inspired, as motivation grasped my young eleven-year-old heart, to propel myself into a deeper sense of spiritual awareness. I became sensitized to the Holy Spirit's call, nudging me to accept Jesus Christ as the Lord and Savior of my life.

I remember that in church when an invitation was given, a group of young people went to the altar, including me, for prayer. I had now embarked on my new found faith-based journey in Jesus Christ. As I got up from the altar, walking back to my seat, there was this overwhelming presence of peace, joy and a sense of being accepted into the family of God.

Chapter 2:

"Back In the Day as a Christian"

As children, we had a practice to attend many Sunday Schools in our community during the course of one Sunday. First, we would attend the Anglican Sunday School in Bellevue Village, and then we would go down to the Gospel Hall Sunday School in Lavington Village. Lastly, we would attend the Church of God of Prophecy Sunday School in my village, Saddlers. There was hardly any transportation, so we had to walk from point A to point B.

Continuing the journey as a new convert, I became a member of the Church of God of Prophecy and began following after Christ. I was eager to develop my new found faith in God. I soon came to realize that this little church, Prophecy, was no ordinary church.

No, and it was not the status quo, regular church either. The Spirit of God moved among us. It was a place where God's Spirit healed. There, lives were transformed, and we experienced spiritual growth, enabling us to fulfill Christ's commission to go into all the world and preach the gospel.

Testimonies of the work that God did among the members were vibrant, encouraging, and authentic. It was a place where we grew from strength to strength.

We were encouraged and had a desire to trust God more and to live holy and righteous lives before our families, our peers, our Pastors, Leaders and God. We were moving from glory to glory.

I have to say that this church was headed by one of the most spiritually discerning women of God I had ever known. She was Pastor Alvira Ible, affectionately called, "Mother Ible". Each time you would enter the doors of the church, she was there praying in supplication. This was always the case, especially if the church was engaged in revival services. In many cases, such revival crusades lasted longer than they were scheduled for. As you walked into the little wooden building, there was an awesome and revered presence of God. So overwhelming was that "presence", one would know something supernatural was going to happen.

If you were already a faithful Christian, you felt so clean and divinely close to God. Or, if you were not saved, you would become so convicted, and felt compelled to give your heart to the Lord. There was an admirable degree of discipline in that environment also. The Spirit of God was in charge. As such, people were inhibited from "chatting" as is the norm in the sanctuary nowadays. And when the altar call was given, you were moved to go to the altar or fall on your knees between the benches in solemn prayer.

In this church of Spirit-filled leaders and submissive members, the Holy Ghost was evident and functioned in His fullest realm to promote spiritual standards based on practical biblical principles. People came from distant villages, eager to witness great manifestations of God's moving, and many got saved, healed, delivered and baptized.

The members of the church were careful, as much as possible, not to commit sin, nor to practice living in sin. To do so meant that you would be called out by Mother Ible who was always in tuned with the voice of the Spirit. He would sure let her know whenever a careless member faltered. And should such a member attend the House of God when the Spirit of God was flowing, this devout Woman of God, under the Spirit's anointing, would call that one out and invite him or her to the altar for prayer. The Holy Spirit would convict any member of sinful acts, especially if he or she was in a leadership position.

Though Mother Ible would not call out the sin or sins committed, she would simply ask the person in question to come to the altar. Should that person refuse, then she would look directly at him or her and say, "Sister, brother, you really don't want Holy Spirit to tell on you. Do you?" A godly conviction would set in. When that individual would eventually go to the altar, she would lead him or her into a prayer of repentance, and only then would the session of service begin or continue, as the case might be.

That is the way we young people were nurtured and trained to live holy lives. We lived in the 'aaaha-ha moment' of God's presence, and we learned to fear Him. It was imperative to pray for forgiveness before going to Church, or personal prayer might have been required at the altar before service started, just in case there were unbecoming things you may have done. Members were so conscious to living right and to be holy.

Further, if you came to church while service was in session, you had to go to the altar for personal prayer, or you would need to pray in your seat, whether by kneeling or bowing of the head while seated. It was not just the norm, but a sign of respect for God's House.

Back in the Day, we revered God's house and honored the leaders that He had set over us. We were hungry for the move of God. We were not satisfied with just being saved, but to be sanctified and filled with the Holy Spirit. It was our ambition to develop our spiritual gifts and talents.

I had become so conscious about preserving my spiritual integrity, that I restrained myself from being seen in a questionable setting with the opposite sex. To do otherwise, it would appear that I was not a serious Christian. Even the very idea of sex was so taboo back then. To be seen alone with the opposite sex, especially if that person was not born again, you would be interrogated not only by leaders of the church, but by the community as well. For me, that stigma alone caused me not to want to engage in any relationship.

Besides, as I was the first girl in my family, all eyes were on me to make good of my life. My parents were strict and proud of me, and my brothers were protective and shared how they felt about me.

17

Many of my peers were either involved in relationships or had become pregnant. So, I dared to be different. I wanted to live up to my family's expectations. Well, not only that, but the older folks of the church held us accountable and responsible as well.

These were "Mothers in Zion" – old spiritual folks like: Sister Joseph, Sister Megnum Caines and Sister Ursilla Brooks (the mother of the renowned Bishop Evan Brooks of Anguilla), Sister Alberta French, Sister Patty Gift and many more elders of the church. They would often ask me, when they met me on the street or when they visited my home: "Sis, are you bearing fruits?" or they would ask, "What is He (the Holy Spirit) saying to you today?" and, "When last have you read His word?" Yes, they kept us in-check with words of encouragement in our walk with Christ.

From this little church in Saddlers produced Pastors like: Pastor Alberta French, though she served for a short tenure, then there were Pastor Phoebe French and Pastor Juana Nelson-Thomas who were instrumental in ensuring that their members lived righteous and holy lives.

A church that propagates the lifestyle of living righteously will most likely produce the same after its own kind. These Leaders lived exemplary lives. They lived truth and demonstrated themselves as uncorrupt, unbiased faithful examples in church and out of the church. They were well respected in the communities and many young people's lives were touched and transformed by the way they lived.

I have to say that even if one was not a born again Christian, after visiting the church or being around one of its members, there would be a certain uneasiness that would almost be convicting. That was how many persons got salvation. The Spirit was alive through righteous living by those who set the examples, letting their light shine.

The comparison between *Christians* **Back in the Day** and some modern-day Christians boils down to one thing. It is letting your light so shine before men, that they may see Jesus living inside of you. This means that your light must be on twenty-four-seven, everywhere you go. Some persons attempt to shine their light in church but outside of the church, that light goes dim. For some folks, when they leave the familiar and travel overseas, that light goes dim. They feel free to indulge themselves in every deceptive thing, until they are back on their home shores. I call such a lifestyle an on-and-off rollercoaster Christian. But remember, the Bible says, that God's Spirit will not always strive with man. One day, such persons may be disappointed while they are on that rollercoaster ride. They may need God— but will not find Him.

We must begin to realize that the unseen eyes of God are still looking out for His people and He is demanding and expecting us, as the church, to be Holy as He is. When emphasis on Spiritual Christian living and teachings are not demonstrated in the church, it is important to note this is the reason why we have compounded, conflicting worldly ideologies becoming the order of the day in modern churches –where everyone has his own erroneous point of view. This is a practical dilemma which the church has been subject to. Conflicting worldly ideologies affect true Christian principles and godly values.

My ardent encouragement to Christians everywhere is to let us begin to clothe ourselves with every piece of the armor of God whereby we are able to resist and to stand against the wiles and cunning craftiness of our adversary. As the word of God tells us that, we do not wrestle against flesh and blood, but against principalities, against powers, against rulers of darkness of this present world, against spiritual hosts of wickedness in heavenly places, Ephesians 6:10-18.

Chapter 3:

"A Respected Christian"

We, young Christians of the community, were greatly respected by many of our younger peers and older folks alike. As a Christian **back in the Day**, we were expected to uphold the convictions that we professed in the lifestyle we possessed. We just didn't talk the talk, but we had to walk the walk – and live it. We had to be committed to our faith in a serious way.

Young people **in the Day** fellowshipped together. We looked out for one another. We studied the Bible together and encouraged one another with scriptures. We did not study the Bible together for the purpose of competing against each other but we were eager to learn more and to become stronger people of God.

In January, 1971, a group of fourteen young people of the community, including myself, were baptized. It was as if our "faith" was sealed that day. We began to follow hard after God from that day onward. There was to be no turning back. By the way, baptism is one of the most rewarding and fulfilling acts one can experience. It testifies to the world that you are determined to forsake sin and rise up from the water, in newness of life, to forever follow after Christ. My baptism was a testimony of my new life to those around me, and I was proud to let the community know that I was baptized – a new me.

I lived about ten minutes away from the church building. One of the activities which preoccupied our village young men was street gambling under the lamppost at evening time. As I would walk to and from church, approaching that area, the youngsters would, all of a sudden, stop their gambling until I passed. After which, they would then continue. In the same vein, if one of them spoke any profane words while I was in the proximity of that area, he would be quick to apologize.

Back in the Day, Christians were respected; but such respect had to be earned. As aforementioned, you had to live the life not just talk about it. Those on-lookers in the neighborhood knew whether you were a real Christian or not.

Back in the Day, young people were drawn to Christ through other young people, and though many of our parents were not saved at the time, they respected the faith enough to make sure their children went to church and Sunday school regularly.

My mother did not become a Christian until later on in her life, but she made sure that my siblings and I went to church. All twelve of us, at the right age, were born again. As my oldest brother, William was the first to lead the way into conversion and water Baptism. Then the rest of us followed consecutively. Devon, though he was yet a young child, also followed in the Way. One by one, the twelve of us got converted. At some point or another, Momma would confirm whether we were at the stage where we were ready to be baptized.

I was proud of my brothers and sisters. Our paths crossed and were connected through one common factor – the Gospel of Jesus Christ. Notwithstanding, unfortunately, some of them have since erred from the faith. I am therefore praying and believing God for the joy of seeing them return to the fold before the return of the Lord.

Back in the Day, young people sought hard after God and we were not ashamed to let others know that we were Christians and we couldn't wait to go to the House of God to tell, share and encourage our peers in the Lord. Young people had a glow on their faces. There was a joy serving the Lord. His peace was ever present, filling our hearts with contentment.

The attributes of peace and contentment were visible to everyone. It showed in our physical demeanor as well as our spiritual outlook. It was through these Christ- like appearances that others wanted to experience what we had. What a mighty God we serve that he would cause His illumination to brighten the countenance of His children.

Back in the Day, Christians were joyful, excited and were easily discerned as children of God by the communities. Wherever we went we were shown respect, and we were not ashamed to testify that we serve a risen Savior.

Chapter 4:

"The Transition of a New Leader"

After Mother Ible passed away, (Pastor Ena Lake served for a one-year period, and was transferred to Newtown Ground Church). However, we were privileged to have yet another devoted and anointed servant of God to be our leader. He was Pastor John Wesley Powell-Freeman, better known as Pastor Powell. Pastor Powell was a no-nonsense man of God. He lived by example. He was a devout father-figure and a stalwart of the Christian faith to many.

He was a spiritual and moral coach to many youngsters in the village, and he didn't minced words in the pulpit. He preached with conviction, and he demonstrated much spiritual fervor handed down to him by Holy Spirit and from Mother Ible. It was as if she 'spat in his mouth', so-to-speak. Taking over the church's leadership, Pastor Powell lived a holy exemplary life before his congregation.

He was a handsome, charming man, and there was always that glow on his face, as if he polished it with oil. But no, it wasn't natural oil, but rather it was the sheen of the Holy Spirit's presence that always loomed over him.

The gait of his walk was a unique one. We referred to him as "Cool Walker". He walked not in a hurry, but yet it was difficult to keep up with his pace. His strides were long and carefully placed. His overall demeanor was graceful, to say the least. We revered him; we were proud of him; and we loved of our beloved Pastor.

I recall the day, Saturday, August 1st 1970, when disaster struck at sea. The Christina ferry, which plied between St. Kitts and Nevis, tragically sank in the channel. Pastor Powell's mother was one of the passengers aboard the vessel. Unfortunately, she perished on that dreadful day. Though he was faced with such loss and grief, it was remarkable that Pastor's demeanor, as a Minister of God, did not change. Instead of expressing his own grief, he comforted others who were grieving themselves for the loss of their family members. He drew no attention to himself, but continued to deal with his flock out of a heart of sheer love and selfless care.

Another remarkable characteristic about Pastor Powell was that, as he preached, he demanded your undivided attention –rightfully so, for the Word of God requires that kind of interest. And, you dare not sleep in God's house while he was ministering the Word. You'd be sure that he would throw some object from the pulpit or have your neighbor sitting close to jolt you out of your slumber.

During my formative years, I have seen many visiting ministers hosted by the Saddlers church. These included persons like Brother Charlie Webb, Brother Doval Ottley, Pastor Steven Liburd, Pastor Arthur Elliott and more. Others would come from neighboring islands that had churches affiliated with Pastor Powell. Some remarkable things happened when visiting Ministers came.

I remember this one Minister in particular, Pastor Arthur Elliott. He hailed from Nevis, and he was the speaker for a 'special night's service. As he preached, at some point during the course of the anointed message, all of a sudden, it was as if the church expanded and floated off into another realm. He instantly began speaking in another language – in tongues.   Wow! It was so dynamic. There were uproars of praise and worship with supernatural manifestation.

What was so fascinating and strange about the moment was that, amazingly enough, people were responding and were being elevated to spiritual consciousness without an interpreter. It was as if those who responded all understood what was being said in another tongue.

It was a charged episode – a supernatural moment that catapulted the church into another level of our Christian walk. Many souls were saved that night. Even to this day, that same overwhelming anointing still hovers over me. Hallelujah! It was a glorious and amazing experience.

Chapter 5:

"A Worshipper is Born"

My journey as a Worshipper began one night in 1971 at the age of fourteen. The church often engaged in weeks of crusades or revival services and, as stated earlier, what was supposed to be a two-week revival, most times turned into six or seven weeks of Holy Ghost-filled services that launched the church into fiery experiences like a rocket from earth to Heaven.

On such occasions, there was standing room only in the small, wooden Saddlers church building that could only house about ninety people or so. But it would be miraculously expanded to hold almost two hundred souls each and every night of the crusade.

On the outside, the yard was always jammed pack with on-lookers who came from neighboring villages to view the excitement inside. Under conviction, many were moved and drawn from the outside to the altar to be saved, sanctified and be filled with Holy Spirit, with the evidence of speaking in tongues. This was an every night occurrence which would go on six long weeks or so. Oh, so amazing and heavenly it was!

It was imperative for new converts to seek to be filled with Holy Spirit after their conversion. Pastor

Powell and the Church Leaders ensured we were properly developed for ministry. Two of the talents that I developed were leading Song Service and Testimony Service. In addition, I would exercise the gift of praying occasionally, and sometimes I would practice learning playing the guitar alongside Brother William French, if Sister Juana Nelson-Thomas was not there.

It was also noticeable, as I led song service, that amazingly my voice would be heard distinctly over the congregation without the use of a microphone. I was told by Pastor's wife, Sister Powell, (deceased) that I had an anointed voice. She would always give me soothing Strepsils lozenges that she carried in her hand bag, and occasionally she would slip two into my hand to aid my vocals, especially when there was a need to practice songs for special occasions.

As I led the singing, the services were inspiring. People would dance in the Spirit and speak in tongues. And they were not ashamed to rise up to testify. No one had to tell anybody to lift hands or plead with them to worship. Worship was a spontaneous, natural thing to do. We loved worshipping God.

I recall on one occasion that the Church invited a nine-member gospel singing group from Jamaica for a two-week revival. From that revival experience, five Caribbean gospel songs stood out and became quite popular all around the region. These were:

(1) "He Saved me and He raise me and that's enough, that's enough, that's enough"

(2) "I Love the Thrill that I Feel When I Get Together with God's Wonderful People"

(3) "Dry Bones connect to, Dry Bones—hear the word of the Lord"

(4) "Soon and Very Soon we are Going to see the King" and

(5) "Get all excited go tell everybody that, Jesus Christ is King".

On the last night of those services with our Jamaican guests, I encountered the most phenomenal, spiritual awakening experience of my life. It was the first time that I had experienced a vision. I remember it vividly:

I was awakened from sleep around three o'clock in the morning and, as my mother claimed, it was something she had never witnessed nor heard of before. I was carried from my bed into the living room. The house appeared to have no roof. There, in the living room, was just an open space, exposed to the sky, and I was dressed in a long white gown.

Everyone else in my family, except my mother, was asleep, and there I was – swirling around the living room, wrapped in a bright, shimmering light. The light hovered over me and surrounded me, as I moved back and forth with both hands lifted shouting, praising and worshipping God. It was awesome – so amazing and breathtaking – and somewhat frightening too, but it was beyond my control. I could clearly see through the open sky, and it was glorious to have the light beaming over me and illuminating the room.

By this time, the rest of the family was awakened. In the supernatural elevation of the moment, I could hear my mother screaming, *"Patsy, Patsy, girl whaa happen' to you?"* I then heard my siblings crying out. When it was all over, the entire family stood in the living room. Some of my siblings were crying, while others were looking scared and dazed. I felt an air of ecstatic joy as I had been enraptured in the presence of God's Holy Spirit. I could not control the spirit of worship that had overwhelmed my being. But my frightened mother kept on asking, *"Girl, whaa happen to you?"* *"Whaa, going on with you?"*

I tried to speak, but I couldn't. In a short span of time, it was deemed that something of a supernatural nature was happening to me. I was speaking in a language of the Spirit, and I knew something wonderful and divine had taken place. My mother was frantically questioning me, but I was not responsive. I was just crying and shaking profusely.

This continued for some time. By now, I could hear noises coming from the outside, as some of the neighbors came to see what all the commotion was about, coming from the Masons' house. I learned afterward that some of those same neighbors claimed to have seen that bright light over our house.

Later that day, my mother decided to take me to the village doctor, as I was still crying and not responding. The doctor looked at me, as he tried to assess what was going on with this little girl. He asked my mother if I had seen something out of the ordinary, or if someone had passed away in the family, or if, per chance, something dramatic had happened in the home. My mother could not confirm any of these. Well, the doctor's last words were, *"Just give her some time and she would be fine."* He didn't give us medication of any sort. He just said, 'give her some time'.

After returning home, I went in my bed and slept for the rest of the day, through the night, and into the next morning. During the night, I had sensed the presence of someone checking on me every once in a while. The next day, I was 'good to go'. I got up and did my house chores took care of my younger siblings and off to school I went. The rest is history.

Chapter 6:

"The Preparation Period"

That same year, looking back in retrospect, I soon realized that God had prepared me for what was to come.

As the oldest girl in the family, my chores every Saturday were to wash clothes, clean the house and iron every one of my younger sibling's school clothes for the entire week. Saturday was a full day of weekend chores. It was a bit overwhelming, and though difficult for me at that tender age, I had to do it – all by myself.

On one such Saturday afternoon, while ironing, two of my sisters and I were engaged in a child play called 'dolly house'. I was the "mommy". My mother had just finished cooking on a three-rock fire place in an outdoor kitchen.

We had already eaten for the evening, but the coals were still lit and, as a practice, we took the opportunity to roast potatoes and corn. But this evening, playing dolly house, I decided to get me a Lactogen milk can and I summoned one of my sisters to get some potatoes and yams for us to 'cook' in the can. While she went to get the vegetables, I put my ironing chores on hold.

I put the Lactogen milk can, containing water, on the three fire rocks – and covered it. While waiting for my sister to come with the veggies, I went back to iron a few more pieces of clothing. Nothing could have prepared me for what was to come next. It was an unbelievable, traumatic and devastating experience.

I went back to the kitchen to continue my task of 'mommy role'. By this time, can you imagine what was going to happen? I could hear the water in the can boiling, so... while leaning over my pan-pot, I tried to lift the cover with the tip of a knife. Woooow! The cover popped off into the air. It was as if all of hell's fury had attacked my face. I had exposed my precious face to a super scalding. The pain was agonizing – excruciating, to say the least. I drop the knife and grabbed my face with both hands. In all the anguish and pain, I scampered out of the kitchen, screaming *"help, help, help!"*

Well, the next thing I knew was that I was rushed to the Joseph N. France General Hospital, almost an hour-and-a- half's drive away. By the time we got there, my entire face and right shoulder were inflamed with terrible blisters. Huge bags of water were hanging down my face. Over 90% of my face was burnt. Both of my eyes were totally shut, and swollen. I spent over a month recovering in the hospital. What an ordeal it was.

But it was in those moments when I felt helpless and alone, having to bathe myself, feed myself, and navigate around my hospital room blindly, that God gave me the opportunity to call on Jesus. I would find myself delving into that supernatural mode which I experienced back in 1971 – that night, under the open skies in our living room. I pleaded with God, asking Him not to let me go blind. I prayed hard that He would heal my face completely.

In the hospital, at age fourteen, all alone with no church to go to, and hardly any visitors, I developed a unique relationship with Jesus.

My family could not come to see me regularly, because they didn't have a car, and both parents worked hard and long. The only time someone would visit me was on a Sunday afternoon. Many members of the church couldn't make the trip either, because of a lack of transportation. There in hospital, confined to loneliness, I understood why God permitted me to go through what I call, **the *preparation period.***

Certainly, it was in that sacred hiding place that I was able to further develop in God. He brought me comfort and miraculous healing both spiritually and mentally.

As a result of this ordeal, I was out of school for seven months, recuperating. When I was able to resume school, I was teased and mocked by my peers as well as many other children. Only a few kind ones empathized with me. Many of them called me "jumbee face" and "scar face."

The burns I sustained had left many black and white patches and scars. At home, I stayed indoors, most of the time, to avoid the taunting and, generally, to avoid contact with anyone in the neighborhood. If I chance to be outside for any reason and noticed anyone approaching, I would quickly rush inside the house.

As I returned to school, I was required to work hard to catch up with the rest of the class. Through all of this, I learned how to connect with God for myself. Every day was a challenge, but every day I prayed, asking God to heal my face. Gradually, He surely did. The doctors were amazed and declared it was a miracle that my eyes were not affected. And my skin, Oh! Thank God it gradually returned to its normal pigmentation. There is just a little area of discoloration on my right shoulder where some light scars are left and are still slowly vanishing.

I give God ardent praise and thanks for His miraculous healing power. Up to this day, every now and then, I find myself going back, through the means of my memory, to that episode in my life, especially when I am facing a situation in which I am most venerable. But oh, the virtue that I draw from that experience, particularly when I am in a worship mode.

I have discovered that I can reflect upon that *period of preparation, as well,* and find my hiding place in God. In moments of turmoil, that reflection becomes my life line, my source of strength, and my connection with God to gain the victory over every adverse situation in my life. It would be as if I'm being transported to another realm – each time. In this realm, I have experienced healing for myself as well for others, and other manifestations of a divine nature. In this realm, I can feast on spiritual goodies and derive spiritual benefits. Memory is a precious gift of God that no adversary can destroy. Through the Spirit, it takes me to a place where I always seek to be.

The scriptures are accurate, of course, when they declare: *"In God's presence there's fullness of joy, at His right hand there are pleasures forevermore"*. I've come to realized that it is in this realm I can do all things, through Christ who strengths me. The Holy Spirit reveals Himself and inspires me to do his bidding. I have discovered that worship is one of the vehicles that propel me into becoming who I am in Him.

The closer we are drawn to God, the more Holy Spirit will be drawn to us to empower us. Another key benefit is the baptism of the Holy Ghost with the evidence of speaking in tongues. It is the key element that will give one power to perform healings and miracles just like Jesus did. Healing is a slow process while miracles are instant. Thank God that my scars were slowly healed and my face was eventually restored.

The bible says, **these signs and wonders shall follow the believers, not believers following after signs and wonders**. It is the Spirit who will administer these signs and wonders to believers. And as one continues in this realm, it will be discovered that other dimensions of the Spirit will be attained as long as the believer walks humbly before the Lord.

If a believer desires to be extraordinary in the Kingdom of God, then the necessary steps must be taken in the Spirit to bring him or her in line with God's perfect plan. No plan of God can be attained without prayer, fasting, worship and reading of God's word. With the desire to excel extraordinarily, one must have a desire to follow after God steadfastly.

Well, it was in my preparation period, through prayer and fasting, that I was given the opportunity to build my relationship in this special way with the Lord. The outcome has been awesome and rewarding. After preparing me, the Lord gave me that opportunity to serve Him in years to come.

It doesn't matter what one's circumstances might be. It is not everyone who will have a Lactogen 'pan pot' explode in their faces like me. But God allows believers to pass through various spells of experiences so that they could be alone with Him. And remember, whatever scars you may pass through, they will be eventually healed in due time. As the old song says, *"some through the water; some through the flood; some through the fire; but all through the blood"*. It's the blood of Jesus, our Savior.

Whatever your lot might be, God is preparing you for your venture. So, utilize your ordeal which will bring you into a closer fellowship with Him through the Holy Spirit. I could have just laid back and allow whatever happened to happen. But instead, I begin to consult with God, to call upon Him, and to prove Him for myself. Indeed, he was preparing me.

I was recently encouraged and blessed by one Minister who was motivated and moved by the Spirit to inspire members of his congregation to get involved in developing themselves in other forms of ministry rather than those of basic church functions. He emphasized how many persons seek only to develop themselves educationally, but sell themselves short when it comes to the bigger picture – to becoming great in God's Kingdom.

God is calling us to a higher level in Him. We cannot move back the hand of time, but we can ensure that we do all within the power and authority that He has given us to bring change to a dying world.

Perilous times are upon us, and they will get harder and harder. If you are not spiritually matured, it will be naturally hard for you to walk with the footmen, moreover to contend with the horsemen, according to   Jeremiah 12:5. Eventually, you might just give in and become weak in your faith, subsequently losing out in making it to the end. You must, therefore, begin to make spiritual preparation, building your faith and storing up spiritual resources for the winter times.

As Ministers and Leaders, we must set a pattern for our people, especially the young people that they can strive and survive spiritually even in isolation, once they are developed and trained. But it seems like most persons are not interested and are only satisfied with going to church. For example, if a survey was to be taken in churches today, you would find only the pastor and his inner circle are comfortable where they are at in the church setting. Invariably, in most church settings, there is no further development or training for a successor outside of what already is.

Our church youngsters need to be prepared and developed to serve in the church. Young people nowadays don't know how to testify, they are not called to do service. They are for the most part shy and are not inclined on their own to serve in the things of the Lord.

As far as service is concerned, there is just the usual rotation of certain sects. No solid foundation is set in place for the future, and hardly any shepherding is done to ensure that young people stay spiritual, other than the usual mundane church programs. But it goes without repetition. In order for churches to grow and be successful, there must be that element of preparation with regard to young people.

As it was in my case, there were church leaders and mentors who coached me in spiritual virtues. Then, with that burn injury that befell me, I was able to shut myself in with God and gain strength, fortitude and inspiration to give him future service. He, along with His ministers of the church, had prepared me to serve Him.

Chapter 7:

"The Virtues of Speaking in Tongues"

Let us put away our programs and agendas, and let us seek to renew our mindsets focusing our attention on bringing ourselves, and the church, in alignment with the Holy Spirit. The Holy Spirit is that agent on earth, the third person of the trinity, whom Christ had sent on the day of Pentecost to guide and direct the affairs of the church. With Him, the church is destined to grow; without Him, the church will stagnate.

In order for the Holy Spirit to guide and direct, he must speak. And often He uses men and women to speak through, with the utterance of tongues.

Let us seek to develop our people so that they would seek to be filled with the Holy Ghost, with the evidence of speaking in tongues, accompanied by other vital, valuable godly experiences. Teachings of the Holy Spirit and His direction is a good place to start, as we become discerning enough to embrace what God wants us to do and what He wants to do amongst us.

I would dare ask the question; how many pastors seek to ensure that their people are developed in this regard? Teachings of the Holy Spirit are so important in the Body of Christ. So, could it be that, this is the reason why some churches have not been victorious as they should be in this 21st century?

Historically, the church has been triumphant in the battles against the enemy because it has allowed the Holy Spirit to fight for it. There was a high regard of the Holy Ghost, or the Holy Spirit, as you may prefer to call Him. Throughout the centuries, He had been in charge. And yes, he spoke. So why are we not seeing great spiritual happenings in our day? Why has the church become so powerless?

By the way, I wish to interject here that there are divine virtues in speaking tongues. Today, the modern church, compared to the real Pentecostal ministries of yesteryear, seem to have deviated from the Spirit's order of speaking in tongues. But there are many vital benefits in tongues.

Tongues represent a heavenly language. As believers, followers of Christ, we should be encouraged to utilize the gift of tongues for our personal spiritual growth. Some virtues that can be experienced by speaking in tongues include: healing, deliverance, revelation, transformation, spiritual growth and so much more. These are the virtues which benefit the work and ministry of the Body of Christ on earth. We must understand that Christ is not here on earth today, but His Body is here to represent Him. He has given His Spirit to believers, and they are charged to operate in the Spirit and occupy until He returns.

Howbeit, there are some modern-day church folks who utter languages for the show. They overextend themselves in speaking in tones which are not cohesive with scripture, and do not benefit the church in anyway.

From my own personal experience, I once asked a question of Prophet Rudolph Morton, a renowned anointed Minister of the Gospel, during a 2009 seminar in St. Maarten. The question on speaking in tongues was: whether it was possible for a minister or member to speak in more than one heavenly language (tongues), at particular times, and for various purposes. He confirmed, "*Yes, the Spirit may use anyone who is yielded to the Lord to speak in tongues for the purpose of healing, deliverances, for worship, during warfare prayers for breakthroughs, or whatever the ministering need might be.*" See? There must be a result. Something must be taking place in the Spirit realm while one is utilizing the Spirit's language in the church.

Tongues are in operation today, and, through them, a significant wealth of spiritual dimension can be achieved in one's life. Contrary to some persons' beliefs, tongues are a vital part of a Christian's makeup for strong spiritual growth. This is a language the devil cannot understand. He knows not what you are saying or praying about. Therefore, he cannot interrupt or abort your prayers made to the Father through the medium of tongues.

If a person is speaking Spanish, or any other language for that matter, and you don't understand what they are saying, it is the same way in the Spirit realm when one speaks in tongues. If he is speaking a message to the church, the Spirit will use an interpreter so that the general church body would clearly get the message.

Another thing to note is that there are many tongues for different administrations of service in the Spirit realm. The Spirit can enable you to be bi-lingual, speaking in two or more tongues. It may be, when you pray for the sick, there's a tongue that is utilized specifically for that purpose. Praying for deliverance, praying directly against evil, warfare prayers or whatever the case might be, the Spirit may gift the speaker with a particular tongue for each one of these ministries. It is the Spirit that administers the tongues as gifts to the ministers who are humbly yielded to the Lord in service.

We should not be forgetting the English tongue, which is a powerful tongue that can elevate and inspire persons individually. However, when you are praying and want a specific outcome, it is sometimes necessary to pray in another tongue, and, of course, it is the Holy Spirit who will cause you to speak in the tongue according to what He is administering.

Like I mentioned earlier, if you speak English, Satan understands your prayers when you pray in English and your human acquaintances understand when you pray in English as well. However, if you do not want any interference or hindrance to your prayers, then it is best to pray in your heavenly language. No devil or human is able to influence, abort or counteract your prayer(s).

Human beings can abort your prayers by doubting or by having a negative attitude towards them. This is a part of the devil's job –

to influence persons or entities to block your concentration and prayers. So, it is only wise for you to develop your tongue language to be utilized as the Holy Spirit gives the utterance. Only God is able to bring to pass whatever you are praying for. He brings results when His Spirit is involved.

Various tongues will come only by your daily dedication and devotion in prayers, fasting, worship, and reading of God's word. They exuberate from a heart and mind that chases after God, wanting more of Him.

I recall one night in a prayer meeting service; a sister began speaking in tongues. As I listened keenly, I realized she was speaking in a Chinese language. I had heard many tongues before, but I had never heard this one. It was amazing! While it sparked my interest, I was hopeful that one day we would be blessed to have some Chinese brothers and sisters in our midst. This is not impossible, for it was the same Spirit that infiltrated the Upper Room when the Day of Pentecost "had fully come".

I long for that day when every language will be heard declaring the will and purpose of God. I seriously believe the reason why we are not seeing Christians taking interest in speaking in tongues is because of the myth that there must be an interpreter to translate what is been said. While there's some truth to this, that very concept is restricting the church from becoming reformed and transformed to a state of unity, or the oneness that Jesus prayed for in John 17:21.

In Acts 2:1-21 bears the account. In the Upper Room on the day of Pentecost, there were no interpreters. The persons who stood by were amazed when they heard their languages being spoken by the apostles and saints who had being praying in the Upper room.

They were the ones who curiously questioned Peter, asking him, how was it that the disciples were speaking in each of their languages.

They were excited to be able to relate with the various languages which were in their native tongues. Though the messages were in several tongues, these visitors who had come from afar could well understand and relate with what the apostles were speaking.

So let us be challenged today to seek to tap into the unknown for the knowledge which God will impart through His Spirit. May we fortify ourselves in the greater dimension that has been laid out for us in order to become complete in all aspects of the Spirit's functioning. We cannot say we are led by the Spirit but still deny His power to speak with His voice through us. God has a work to do through men and women of the church.

Chapter 8:

"Benefits of a Developed Christian"

Looking back as a young convert in my church in Saddlers, St. Kitts, we were tested in our spiritual growth. Systematically, all who were converted were required to testify of their experiences with God.

And really, we were all excited to go to the House of God to tell how this new- found faith was working. We were eager to be involved in track distributions, open air services and group home visits where we were developed in ministries, gifts and talents for the Lord. In the Saddlers church, we sat with the elders, senior brothers and sisters, to learn more. Besides, we encouraged one another and played a prominent role in assisting the weaker ones.

Many times, as a new converts in Christ, when testimony service was in session, we were indebted to testify. In most cases our testimony was like a standard recital. Those who had recently gotten saved would say: "Thank God for saving me and keeping me alive." And they'd quickly sit back down. Others, who were in the faith for a while, would repeat the first couple lines of an inspirational song, and then add: "My only aim and desire is to continue serving Him until He comes or calls me home." Then there were the more mature ones who would take it a little further with more substance. I remember that when it was my turn to testify, as a young convert, all I could say while crying, was: "Jesus wept" and I would sit back down quickly. My goodness, it was so overwhelming and yet so exciting.

However, because of one's desire to grow and learn how to testify more effectively, we would get into groups or with a close church friend and practice what we would say during the next testimony service. And, yes, as the Holy Spirit began to do His work in us, we overcame the struggles of public speaking and became authentic in our testimonies.   Those were beautiful, passionate and precious memories.

As developing Christians, we did not stop at learning how to testify, but we moved on learning how to pray, even as Jesus thought his original disciples. We also learnt how to lead song service, testimony service, how to preach and how to moderate a service. We were in training all the time, for one thing or another.

While we were being trained, we would be sent to conduct a prayer meeting or to moderate a home visit. And, we were required to report what was done. We had to give account of our progress. We were expected to state how many souls were saved, and to describe the overall quality of the reception from the people whom we visited. It was like what Jesus did in the Bible as he sent out His disciples two by two, except, in our case we were sent out in small cell groups.

When it came to open air services, we would walk miles and miles to the location, into another village. As transportation was scarce and the church didn't have a bus, we were required to walk back and forth every time. It was a joy walking together, singing on the way to church. It would take us about an hour or more to get to some destinations.

We had spiritual endurance, though, and we were happy to see others come to the faith.   And like I said, though the journey was long, back and forth, it gave us pleasure to sing jubilantly while talking about spiritual things as we went.

We would be speaking of Jesus like the men on the road to Emmaus, until they finally met up with Him. In talking about Him, we, as it were, encouraged His presence among us, and when we arrived at the church meeting, our hearts would be ready to receive the ministry of His Spirit through worship and to hear a sermon of Jesus from His word. The Spirit and presence God would precede us, and the grounds would be prepared and watered for the seeds of the word that would be planted in the hearts of the hearers.

Chapter 9:

"Leaving Home at Nineteen"

In 1976, when I was eighteen, almost nineteen, I travelled to Anguilla. There I spent two months with a veteran Mother of the faith, Pastor Virginia Vanterpool. I then travelled to the neighboring island of St. Maarten where I was hosted by another great Mother of Zion, Evangelist Mary Salomon. She was a landmark benevolent character in the community of Cole Bay, who had help to pioneer the Church of God of Prophecy there.

I remained in St. Maarten for three years before returning to my homeland St. Kitts for a short visit. A group of my Christian friends accompanied me on the trip aboard the popular hydrofoil ferry, Bianca.

When I arrived home that day, my father was so elated to see me. He thought it was a good thing to go parading me around at many of the places where he hung out with his drinking buddies. I rejected the idea of walking with him to these obscene places. Besides, I was very tired from the trip and I just wanted to rest.

However, my mother convinced me to go along with him, which I hesitantly did. As he introduced me to his comrades, he would exclaim: "Look at my daughter, man. See how she keeps up herself in St.

Maarten?" I definitely was not charmed by his bragging, for it was more of an embarrassment to me. Though he drank a lot, I regarded my father with a certain degree of grace. And I knew from my growing-up years that his friends respected the family, including me as well.

I began to realize how proud he was of his little girl who had gone abroad and had kept herself pure. So, I loosened up and breathed easier, but I couldn't wait for this showdown to be over with.

Remarkably, in St. Maarten I had bought our first television for our home in St. Kitts. It was a red Zenith TV. It was imperative that I purchase this TV, as my siblings and I, along with other children in the neighborhood, used to gather on the porch of our School Master's house, the Edwards' family, to watch our favorite TV shows. Now we had our own black and white Zenith TV, and could invite children of the neighborhood to come over to our house to watch their favorite shows.

Returning to St. Maarten, I continued to live at Sister Solomon's. There were two other church sisters who lived with me. The church was next to our residence, which shared the same yard. Naturally, as church members, living so close to

God' house, we were required to go to church each time the doors were opened.

Immediately after the preacher would finish preaching, however, or sometimes when he was almost through, we who lived in the vicinity of the church would team up with an older sister and sneak out of the service. Our aim was to get home in time so we could watch the popular TV show, *"Dark Shadows"*. Well, I admit that was not Christ-like, but we irresistibly did it, hoping that we wouldn't be caught by Sister Solomon and singled out for our "disrespect".

As time went by, I became very much attached to the work and ministry of the Cole Bay church. The church's leader, Pastor Elvira Hodge, was very spiritual. She was a serious personality, but very benevolent and sweet, to say the least.

I felt so much at home among the Cole Bay church brethren. I enjoyed the camaraderie and the great atmosphere of harmony and fellowship that existed there. Soon, my interest and passion for singing grew and developed to enhance the worship sessions. Eventually, I, along with three other sisters, namely: Rosie Lake, Sheila Connor and Diane Carty, started a church quartet. The record would show that we lifted the level of worship in the Cole Bay congregation.

Later, Pastor Elvira Hodge gave way to the leadership of Bishop George Connor. Under his ministry, our quartet continued to function, in the Spirit, with our harmonious singing. It was highly rewarding for us to render praises as we led the congregants in worship to the Lord. All who heard us in that era were touched by our singing ministry, and the church in general gave us great encouragement.

As time went on, I had gotten married and began to raise a family. The church was a central part of our lives. By this time, the leadership had changed hands again, as Bishop Connor was transferred elsewhere, making way for the ministry of Bishop David Rogers. It was a pleasure for me to work with these humble men of God. It was not long before Bishop Rogers was transferred and Bishop Michael Greenaway took over the leadership of the Cole Bay church.

I can testify that my association with the Cole Bay church marked a significant milestone in my spiritual life. I will always cherish the memories of the fellowship that I experienced there. The work of the ministries which I was involved in at that church enabled me to grow and mature in Christian service.

Chapter 10:

"A Call to Serve"

Life's circumstances had dictated that I leave St. Maarten, 1997, and move to Anguilla with my husband, James, and our three sons. In July of 1998, I established a local non-denominational gospel singing group, of which I was Director. The group comprised mainly of youths. Later on, James joined us as Co-Director. By this time, the group had grown to about thirty-seven members, and we went by the name *"Melodies from Heaven"*. The youngsters were excited about singing on stage.

The name *"Melodies from Heaven"* is actually the name of a song sung by Kirk Franklin and The Family. In order to be legal about it, James wrote to Kirk's agent, Gospel Centric, requesting permission to use the name to adapt it as the name for our singing group. Permission was readily granted when the agent learnt of our intent.

"Melodies from Heaven" was a vibrant bunch of enthusiastic young people who enjoyed receiving many invitations to sing at various churches, concerts and engagements in Anguilla, as well as in St. Maarten. Members' ages ranged from twelve to forty and over. The majority of group members comprised of young people from various denominations, all around Anguilla.

We performed with well- known artists in St. Marten, like Hellen Hart and her husband, Neville "Fatts" James, of Melody Recording Studio, where our first CD entitled *Shekinah Fills This Place* was produced.

Having being in ministry most of my life, the Lord opened the door for me to serve as Cofounder of The No-Walls Church of Hope, which was established in 2007. On June 4, 2008, I was ordained as a licensed Minister of Worship. At the same time, James and I were ordained as licensed Pastors of the church. The church grew by leaps and bounds over the period of seven years. So great was the growth, that we had to relocate to a larger edifice in 2012. Souls were saved, healed and delivered, as the Lord was magnified, glorified and lifted up.

The manifestation of the supernatural glory of God was in operation in the ministry. Many persons and entire families had joined the church after they were healed. They were then taught and developed in the faith. The church was energetic and on fire for the Lord. Besides, though persons were not members of the ministry, in particular, they would be sent or call for prayers and appointments would be set for them to come in for special prayer sessions.

The Youth Department of the church quickly grew to over 56 youths. Our youths were trained in etiquette, and systematically taught the rules and conventions that would regulate their social and professional behavior in society. For example, young men were specifically trained to respect and honor their female partners, and how to honor seniors. As for the young ladies, they too were trained how to honor seniors, and how to respect their male counterparts. They were taught the three principles of Etiquette: Respect, Consideration for others and Honesty.

At the church, we featured wholesome sleepovers for the youth, and they were trained to stay away from each other's sleeping quarters. These young people enjoyed the ambiance of youth development at every Friday night session, and they were eager to bring along others with them to share in the various events.

I am so proud of how many of these young people having developed and governed themselves in society. Over the years, through the church, I was instrumental by providing school supplies to many children from kinder-garden to high school age, from 2008 to 2016.

As an ardent pioneer and pastor, it was my spiritual duty to ensure persons walk up rightly before God and to be the example, just as I had been mentored during the course of my early Christian years. Though none of us are perfect, this should not limit us or inhibit us from setting high spiritual standards and goals. As Christian leaders, it should be our tasks to find ourselves involved in Christian service, no matter how menial it may be.

The Lord has our reward in store. We might not have the privilege of seeing great returns from our investments here and now, but as we set our affection on things above, and not on things of the earth, we will ultimately be content with the fruits of our labor.

During the tenure of my service in the No-Walls Church of Hope, I saw to it that the church was advancing and lives were being spiritually affected. But so, too, did the enemy "advance" his mission. He crept in and created chaos among us through some of leaders and members, who had become disrespectful, contrary and careless. There's a saying that goes, "the majority rules". Well, that applied in this case, and the rest is history.

Chapter 11:

"Accountability of God's Servant"

Many believers hold the view that if a person tells of God's acts of healing, deliverance, dreams, visions and shared prophecies, etc., that they are boasting. Some persons who hear them telling the good news might respond by saying: "It's not about you"; or "You're full of self". Literally, they would want to shut you up.

Many of us had been told that while functioning in our respective ministries. We were made to feel guilty for telling of divine visions and dreams, or for otherwise sharing the experiences of what God has done through us and for others.

All throughout the Bible, stories are told of how Jesus worked many miracles everywhere He went. It was for the purpose of working for Him that He sent out the disciples two by two to accomplish great works and to report the same. We read in the Bible of many great feats that men and women of God achieved through His Holy Spirit at work in their lives.

So why should anyone, try to discourage one who testifies of how God performs His work and manifests His power through them? Before Jesus went back to the Father, He proclaimed that he had been doing great works, but then He said, "Greater works than these shall you do, because I go to the Father," according to John 14:12. And, in going to the Father, Christ has sent His people the power through the Holy Spirit to do great works for Him.

It was Jesus Himself who promised: "You shall receive power after the Holy Ghost is come upon you, and you shall be witness unto me in Jerusalem, in Judea and Samaria and unto the utmost parts of the earth," according to Acts 1:8. The Holy Spirit empowers one to work for Christ and enables His servants be witnesses of His mighty acts.

The works you do and the experiences you share give glory to God as you are empowered by the Holy Spirit. The works you do indicate that you are a disciple of Jesus. That is the reason why you were commissioned in first place – to work. The work you do shows that you are fulfilling Kingdom agenda, and the life you live in Christ Jesus speaks of who you are in Him.

Having the "title" Christian simply for the sake of having a title without works, does not bring glory to God or to His Kingdom, but it only appeases oneself. (James 2:14-20) And, since we are His workmanship in the earth, then it only means that we are His offspring. As such, we should live lives so that He can perform His will on earth through us. And there should be nothing to deter us or discourage us from sharing and telling of His mighty acts.

Does God give power to certain classes of people only? Or do some Christians take it upon themselves only to serve where they are based? I was listening to a gentleman on radio once who referred to some white ministers who preach "white Christianity" versus black ministers who preach a "black Christianity". I do not mean to be mistaken for being a racist of any sort, but here is what I have observed: that in white congregations, mainly in the US and Europe, the members reach out with ministries outside of the confines of the church building. By enlarged, they promote the Kingdom of God outside of the "four walls".

However, the majority of black church leaders, and especially in the Caribbean area, tends to keep their ministries focused within the church buildings. They exert control over their congregations. It is somewhat like an image of slavery, as they do not send their prominent members forth and bless them in new ministries like Jesus did with his disciples, making other disciples of men.

Over the years, I have been told this by "church folks": "Look Sister, it's not about you, it's about God" – trying to shut me up and make me feel guilty. They try to enslave and confine the people of God to the dictates of their control and would want to make me feel like I am boastful in their eyes and would even say among themselves that I was full of pride.

Well, if we can't share or testify what God has done for us – or through us, without being labeled as being boastful, and if we fail to promote the gospel so that men and women may hear it – whether on the highways or on the byways – then how is God supposed to get the glory?

Again, typically, anyone who ventures to work for God outside of the "black" church gets some degree of opposition from "church members". But such opposition should encourage zealous persons to work for the Lord with even more passion, instead of discouraging their endeavor.

Nowadays, people are not telling about great works of God simply because in many churches there's nothing progressive to tell about. And if one dares to have reason to break the status quo, he or she would be labeled as being "full of self".

Church people need to stop it. We need to allow persons with potential for service to "big up" God in our churches, schools, homes, communities and on the streets. People of God, go tell! You are responsible and accountable to be a witness for Him. Tell what God has done for you and be bold enough to tell of the work that He is doing through you. Stop giving credit to outside entities that operate in other forms of religion or denominations. Do the work as a servant of God. Be accountable to the Lord in the task that He has given you, and just see to it that all the glory goes to Him.

Sharing and telling of the goodness and love of God means we are encouraging and supporting our Christian fellowmen. Testifying of God's acts and of His gracious nature would help the unbeliever to believe; and it will foster spiritual growth among church folks. Oh, how we need to get back to Bethel – to how it used to be. We must be inclined to serve the Lord without the fear of intimidation.

We need to allow our lights to shine. The power of God would flow through us only when we submit to Him. Christ has saved us, and as Christians we ought to be accountable to bring others to a saving knowledge of the precious son of God. As Christians, we have a duty to win souls in the Kingdom. As Christians, we are accountable to God to pray prayers of deliverance and see those who are bound liberated by His invincible, chain-breaking power.

Let us allow the power of God to flow and touch whomever He may. In that way, more souls would be born into His kingdom, and more people would be healed, set free, and delivered. Yes, the church needs to take the limits off of God's people who are walking in obedience to His will. Church leaders must allow God's will and purpose be realized in the earth. When this is done, God's supernatural works will be manifested, and the end-time agenda of his kingdom will be accomplished.

Chapter 12:

"Taking Flight into the Supernatural"

We have Pastors, Evangelists, Bishops, Apostles, Deacons, Elders, Teachers and Leaders – the full package and more. We claim to have the "Five-Fold Ministry", but hardly is there any evidence of the power of God manifesting among us. Modern day churches have deviated from the standards of the original Church which Christ established upon Himself as its foundation.

Today, many churches have become impacted with familiar spirits and have become a breathing ground for jealousy, stagnation, infighting and spiritual incest right in the House of God. "How spiritual incest" Did you ask it? Sure! When a minister would make sexual advances towards a female member to whom he is a spiritual father, then that spells "spiritual incest".

But it is time that we invoke the Spirit of God to assist us in breaking those curses that has kept us bound for so long. God is looking for righteousness among His people and He expects men of God to uphold standards of chastity, purity, and integrity.

We, the people of God must repent – every one of us, from the pulpit down to the door. We, the church needs to show the world that we are prepared to change our familiar ways. We must repent of sins of commission and sins of omission. While acts of unrighteous have been committed, there are also good things which the church leaders omit that would be otherwise beneficial to God's people.

For example, it is evident that some church leaders, whether pastors, teachers or deacons, have the tendency to ridicule persons to whom God have given gifts. Instead of helping to develop such persons, some church leaders make the mistake of omitting paying attention to those persons with the gifts. They often say that there's no need for such gifts in the church today— "those days are over", they say.

Let me make this clear: In every generation God has a man or a woman to lead a nation and to tell that nation what He, God, is saying. It does not matter whom he chooses as long as that individual is connected to Him through the Holy Spirit. It's no wonder there are no clear-cut messages or direction from God, the likes of what Moses and so many other prophets delivered in "Bible times". I would interject here that evidently, there is spiritual famine in our churches and sensitive members are hungry for more of God.

Some churches, or persons, who claim that there's no need, in our dispensation, for men and women after the similitude of Moses, Paul, Esther, Elijah, Jeremiah or Daniel, ends up suffering from divers' spiritual deprivation.

People of God, let's wake up and seek God's face. We have become too sentimental with God's word, mixing it with religion, our own selfish will, and fleshly ideologies. We have omitted adherence to the authentic and rightly divided word of God.

As a concerned believer, with a mandate to pray for the nation of Anguilla, since 2014, I began asking God questions like I have done many times before. But the last answer He gave to me was very troubling and frightening. And, the scenario is as follows:

The Holy Spirit woke me up, and right away I had this great sense that we, the church, is in trouble – trouble of our own making. Here is the trouble: We often quote the scripture in 2 Chronicles 7:14. Well, we need not only to turn and repent, as Israel needed to, but in this age we have become a church that is none responsive to Holy Spirit. The trouble is that we have become religious rather than righteous. We are not sensitive to hearing from God, and there's hardly any quickening of the Spirit of God to convict us of sin and wrong.

The troubling answer continued: The Spirit said that when the Church lacks spiritual fervor, it becomes lukewarm and soon it becomes cold. Then, every realm of society will be affected. This is the state of the church globally.

When the church has lost its fervor or its "salt", then Governments would be in trouble; political factions would arise and wreak havoc in societies; homes and schools would be in trouble; businesses would be struggling and become bankrupt; and communities at large would be facing chaos. Confusion will flood men's hearts and fruits of greed, hatred, jealousy and acts of violence and crime will be taking over the senses of mankind. All this is what the Spirit said.

So, I said: "Lord, I know the church has been on and off, and many times we have seemed to find our way back through 'revivals and crusades' and such, but it has never been like this before," I said. "It has gotten worst."

The Spirit confirmed my observation, agreeing with the Word, which says: "Because iniquity has abounded the love of many has gone cold." This is where I, myself, made it a point to "get back to Bethel", as I admonished earlier. And it was in that moment when God showed me a comparison between **modern day climate-change and the modern-day decline of righteousness. The _decline of righteousness_, yes!**

This brought to mind how Abraham began to bargain with God about how many _righteous_ people could be found in Sodom and Gomorrah. Let me say to Anguilla, my nation, as well as the regions beyond: This "trouble of our own making" is indeed troubling. I am, therefore, appealing to our church Pastors, Ministers, and Leaders – regardless of your denomination – as long as you bear the name of Christ, as long as you carry a title for Jesus, then we must come together and repent of sins. Now is the time to seek the face of God, and turn from our wicked ways, according to 2 Chronicles 7:14.

These are critical times. We are living in the last days. It may seem as if there is nothing much we can do; however, that doesn't mean we should just lay down arms and make no further attempt to rescue the souls of man.

But this all-out rescuing operation must first begin with us, as God's Church –the Body of Christ. Once the rescuing operation is initiated, the Spirit will propel the church to rise and to take its flight into a new direction, exploring supernatural spiritual dimensions.

God is waiting for new desires and changed hearts in order to fulfill his promises to us. However, while the Church maybe transitioning through these times, Jesus Himself stated to Peter, in Matthew 16:18, that, the relationship which existed between them both was like a rock upon which He would build His church. And He further stated that the gates of hell will not prevail against His Church. Yes, there is hope, but we the Body of the Church must do our part to ensure that we stay on course in living righteously until Christ is ready to ultimately rescue us from this world.

Prelude to Chapter 13

On December 4, 2012, I was commissioned as a Prophetess by the late Prophetess Aster Allen. She was my mentor, and an inspiring, anointed woman of God. It was her husband, Apostle Elmead Allen, along with the late Apostle Maycil Roberts, who were my main sources of support.

I must make mention that it was unfortunate to lose both Prophetess Aster and Apostle Maycil, who were responsible for my mentoring and training in the Prophetic. They were the bridges to my ministry, but suddenly succumbed to death, in close proximity.

I must mention as well, that, Pastor Ambrose Richardson, (deceased) was a man of great wisdom. He too, played a prominent role as mentor in my younger years. This great man of God gave James and I counsel as we embarked on the No-Walls Church of Hope Ministries, and he was always ready to share words of encouragement to me.

Let history record that Apostle Maycil Roberts was the first and only resident Apostle on Anguilla in her day. She was then followed by Apostle Elmead

Allen, who, by the way, is a great teacher of the doctrine of the "Five-Fold Ministry".

I am determined, by the grace of God, to allow the Lord to continue to use me to fulfill His kingdom agendas, all to His glory and honor. I want more of Him, and I am encouraged to help anyone who has a desire to use their gifts and talents for His glory. The road of the prophetic is not an easy one, but ultimately, it will be worth it all.

In the next Chapter, where there are accounts of healings and deliverance, some names of persons will be mentioned, and readers have my blessings to speak to these persons for verification. However, in other instances the experiences will be described, but names will be withheld. All in all, I give God thanks for preparing and allowing me to surrender and avail myself to be used by Him. All the glory and praise be to Almighty God.

When we begin to realize the will and purpose of God for our lives, we will change course to fulfill our calling in Him. We are His workmanship in the earth. Our hands and feet should be tools to build up the kingdom. Our bodies are the dwelling places of His Spirit. We must be serious and faithfully play our part in His kingdom, for at the end of the day, we want to hear from our Master "well done" when He returns to take us home. He will say, "Well done good and faithful servant," only if indeed we are faithful. He will then commend us: "You have been faithful over a few things; I will make you ruler over many things. Enter into the joys of the Lord," Matthew 25:21.

It is important to keep in mind that the work you do here on the earth will speak for you, and you will surely reap your just reward in Heaven. Just don't live to go to heaven alone, but you must be desirous to take somebody with you. Then you will be assured that the work you do for God will be counted worthy and valuable. "Don't go to heaven alone, take somebody with you," goes the old familiar song.

It is evident that throughout history, God has anointed the less influential and the unqualified to fulfill His earthly mission. He has most times, chosen the least likely, and lowly persons whom He empowered and assigned as His instruments. He uses them as He chooses. He gives ordinary people His heavenly mantle and set them forth for "His Majesty's Service".

When the Prophet Elijah left this earthly realm, being miraculously caught up into the Heavens, he left his mantle (garment) behind as a source of anointing for the ministry that his mentee Elisha would pursue. When mighty warriors of God die, or leave this earthly scene, God rises up successors and bestows upon them virtues in similitude to those who have gone on before them. In essence, He provides for them an anointing or a mantle that will cover their ministry and produce divine success.

Spiritual mantles are reserved for anyone in the Body of Christ who is serious about rendering service to God. These mantles are, as it were, waiting to be accessed, while believers, who would be assigned to God's work as stewards, make themselves available for supernatural pursuits in God's service. It is important to realize that just as God is waiting to usher out mantles, the earth is longing to be delivered by those to whom the mantles would be presented. Are you ready to access Heaven's covering in order to carry out supernatural acts of God so that you may fulfill your destiny? I pray that if you are zealous enough to be active in the Spirit realm, that God would bestow a mantle of His anointing upon you.

The mantle is a special endowment of the Holy Spirit that gives kingdom leaders an advantage over secular leaders. Kingdom leadership involves a radical change in one's thinking, and it is characterized by a close relationship with the Holy Spirit. These leaders who carry mantles are continually renewing their minds to spiritual truths and experiencing supernatural happenings.

Mantles are not just physical capes or a cloak, as some may think. A mantle represents your gift – the call of God on your life.

With a humble heart, and as an ardent Minister of Worship, a Pastor, and Prophetess of the Kingdom of God, I am moved to share and to tell of the many wonderful, miraculous experiences wroth by the power of the Almighty God in many lives, mainly across the Islands of Anguilla, St. Kitts, St. Marten, the United States of America and the UK.

The experiences that I am about to share are incredible, but they are authentic testimonies and stories that are truthful. They can be confirmed and verified by the Editor of this book, James Harrigan, who had been with me in ministry at the No-Walls Church of Hope. Many other healings and deliverance still continue to occur.

Chapter 13:

"Healing Power, Deliverance and Prophetic Unction"

In 1973, at the age of 16, my hometown church in Saddlers Village St. Kitts was conducting a night of spirited testimonial service, when I witnessed the behavior of a brother of the church who was possessed with evil spirit. He began tearing off his clothes, rolling around on the floor, and his tongue was pitifully hanging out of his mouth.

As he rolled around vigorously, I was empowered by the Holy Spirit to go over him and blocked his legs between my feet in order to prevent him from tossing around continually.

As he was under the influence of that demonic attack, it seemed like he was choking. Then, under the influence of the Holy Spirit, I was empowered with the courage to slap his tongue back into his mouth. The church then went into a season of prayer for his deliverance. It did not take too long before God answered, manifesting His power to deliver this brother who had been repeatedly warned by the pastor about his uncomely habits.

In any case, that particular night he was miraculously set free of his oppression. Besides, he was emboldened to give his testimony, in which he thanked God for breaking the chains that had him bound for so long. He repented from his acts of stealing and was subsequently sentenced to prison for a shorter period. Thank God for his amazing deliverance. Thank God, too, for allowing him to get a relatively brief prison sentence, which could have been many years. To God be the glory!

In 1997: I started working with the Government of Anguilla and worked in various departments. I was soon inspired by the Holy Spirit to send letters to Government officials and to encourage them to acknowledge the Lord who would direct their paths in the leadership of Anguilla.

Government Ministers such as the Hon. Hubert Hughes, the Hon. Victor Banks, the Hon. Edison Baird and the Hon. Albert Hughes were all recipients of my prayers and my encouragement to acknowledge God so that He would direct their paths for their success in government.

In 1999: I told James of a vision I saw where Anguilla would be hit by a hurricane. In the vision, I saw boats in The Valley area (the capital of Anguilla), transporting people back and forth. In the vision, I saw people jumping out of their homes. This took take place with the well-known

1999 Lenny flooding in The Valley. The rest is history.

In 2001: I prayed for James who was having a persistent pain in his chest. He had seen doctors in Anguilla and St. Maarten, but without relief. As I laid my hand on the area, and prayed for him, he was miraculously healed. Again, I prayed for an ailment in one of his ears that lasted for two weeks. Again, through those prayers, he was divinely healed. To God be the glory!

In 2002: One night, I told James I was awoken from a vision in which Saddam Hussein was about to attack the US. Well, we laughed about it, and James was comical enough to tell me that I went to sleep with my belly too full. The next morning, at about 5:30, while I was in the kitchen cooking, I heard him shouting, calling: "Pats, Pats come see this! Come see this! Just like you were saying!," It was breaking news on NBC that, indeed, Saddam Hussein was on TV threatening to attack America.

Saddam Hussein compared his threat to the treatment which was shown of a little white puppy being gassed up in a cage by one of his soldiers. We all know how that went down in the conflict between Iraq and the U.S. History later revealed that in 2003 both nations went to war.

It was reported that Saddam Hussein's sons, Uday and Qusay, were killed that same year by U.S. troops, and later on December 30, 2006, Saddam himself was eventually hanged by an Iraqi Special Tribunal, under the Bush Administration. The rest is history.

In 2005: Our gospel singing youth group, *"Melodies from Heaven"*, received an invitation to participate in a Gospel-fest celebration in St. Marten. There, we had the privilege of meeting with some renowned artists from America.

It was at that time that we learned of the sad news that our former landlord and brother in Christ, Basil Lewis, of St. Marten, was near death. He was operated on due to prostate cancer and was eventually sent home as doctors could no longer do anything more to help him.

James and I decided we would go to visit the family. To our surprise, when we got there he was hooked up to several pieces of medical apparatus to help keep him alive. As he laid there with his eyes rolled back and puffing, he was unable to move. It was as if any moment he would be ushered home to be with his Lord. I was moved with compassion, and my heart broke to see my faithful brother who was such a strong, vibrant man. As a contractor, he had built many houses. He even did some work on our dwelling house in Anguilla and worked on government projects in St. Maarten. But now, he was lying there helpless.

So as usual, James ministered the word to him, while I engaged in worship and prayer. While in the mode of songs, I heard the Holy Spirit speaking to me clearly. He said to have Brother Lewis lifted in a sitting position on the bed, and that I must lie across the bed in the back of him as he was held in a sitting position. With that, I obediently laid across the bed, prayed, and rebuked the spirit of cancer. Then we laid him back down.

As we continued in fellowship, the Spirit said to me to tell his wife to go get a glass of room temperature water and give him to drink. You must understand, lying across his bed sounds crazy enough, but to give him water at room temperature? I could see James and Sister Lewis looking at me as if I had lost my mind. The truth is that, I too, felt "crazy", and up to this day, I laugh to myself when I reflect upon it. But we know that

'God works in mysterious ways his wonders to perform'.

It was certainly amazing, but I was determined and anxious to see the power of God manifested. I obeyed the Holy Spirit. Sister Lewis gave him the water to drink. The room was charged with the very presence of God's anointing and I heard the Holy Spirit say, "*Tell Brother Lewis that in three days he will be up and eating.*"

We came back to Anguilla the following day, and it wasn't until a week later we got a call from Sister Lewis telling us that Brother Lewis was up, just as the Lord had said, eating like a bull. That was not just good news, but it was *great* news to our ears. We therefore decided to go back to St. Marten the next weekend for a visit.

As we entered the yard in Cape Bay, there was Brother Lewis sitting outside on his porch eating. What a joyous moment of rejoicing it was. Before leaving, we prayed, and here comes the Holy Spirit again: "Tell Brother Lewis that in three weeks he would be back in church praising God." With joyous anticipation, I announced to him and his wife what the Spirit had said.

Well, it must have been close to a month later, that we began wondering how the family was doing. James called, and it was good, good news. Brother Lewis himself answered the phone, and he told us that, indeed, three weeks after I gave him the Spirit's promise, he went out to church at the Church of God of Prophecy in Weymoth Hills. According to him, it was a time of refreshing and rejoicing for the church to see him alive and back in the House of God. That is God's glory, y'all – not ours. God had generously allowed Brother Lewis to spend three more years here on earth before calling him home. It was after the third year that he passed away.

In 2006: I prayed for Mr. Alpheus Fleming, the father of a former coworker, William Fleming, of the Keys, Island Harbor. Mr. Fleming, too, was operated on and sent home to die, but God healed him and raised him up. James and I were privileged to witness him "tying the knot" even at a ripe age, with his longstanding beloved fiancée Bernice, whom we affectionately call Bernoo. He, too, was miraculously healed, and he was able to live happily with his wife for some years before passing away.

In 2007: The late Sister Lena Gumbs of South Hill, met James and me one day and told us that we needed to go and pray for Sister Doreen Richardson of West End. Incidentally, some time had passed and we did not avail ourselves to visit her, until we encountered Sister Lena again. She asked if we went to see Doreen. We apologized to her, and after praying about it, and shortly after we decided that we will go, and so we did.

There again, the Spirit of the Lord revealed Himself. Doreen was a beautiful young lady, but now she was quite sickly, feeble and frail. The Spirit told me to get her a glass of room temperature water, as well. After she drank it, I prayed fervently. Doreen was miraculously healed and is still alive today. To God be the glory for the great things He has done.

In 2007: Bishop David Rogers informed us that a member of the Hodge's family in The Cove was sick and was in need of prayer. He was visiting from Texas for a short while. After fervently praying for him, God graciously healed him. He returned to the U.S. as a healed man. Again, to God be the glory.

In 2008: It was the first miracle that took place at the No-Walls Church of Hope, upstairs of the English Rose Restaurant in Anguilla. As church was in session one Sunday morning, and as I was leading worship, a young boy, about 14 years old, was sitting at the front when suddenly, he collapsed in his seat.

Some of the members became worried, and in particular, one gentleman became so irate, insisting the need to rush the boy to the hospital.

I was not so much worried, for I knew that we were in God's House and He would intervene. As I quickly analyzed the situation, I realize the importance to trust God to restore and revive the child. I was not going to miss this precious opportunity to prove the God we serve. I was convinced we had nothing to lose, but that God had all the praises and glory to gain.

So, inspired by the Holy Spirit, I prayed fervently to God for him. Suddenly, he regained consciousness, sat up and stayed focused for the duration of the service. The service ended on a high note, and the atmosphere was charged with hilarious praises. We were grateful for the miracle and gave uncontrolled "crazy" praises unto God. It was so phenomenal to see The Father at work. That young boy was miraculously healed by the power of the Almighty God!

In 2009: My sister, Joyce, and I went to St. Kitts for our brother Eric's wedding, at my hometown church in Saddlers. On the morning of the wedding, it began to rain with fierce lightning and thunder. We were thinking about postponing the wedding due to the inclement weather. However, I was moved to pray and rely on the promise of God to answer. God miraculously stopped the rain and out came the sun. Wow! Such an amazing God we serve. Glory to His wonderful name!

In 2009: Bishop David Rogers again called us one day and told us of a particular situation of this family. He asked that we go and pray for Brother Tony Proctor's wife, Mervette. We went at their home in Cauls Bottom, one evening, and passionately prayed for her. She too was miraculously healed of a serious condition. Mighty is our God!

In 2009: One of our neighbors, Sister Lena, of Wattaces, had a problem with her lower lip and had seen many physicians, but to no avail. One could see her discolored, lip from afar off. One night she came to our prayer meeting at the church, upstairs English Rose. I prayed fervently for her, and she too was healed. Again, to God be the glory!

In 2009: I went to the Hospital, as requested by Sister Janet, a sister of the church, to pray for her friend, who was seriously ill. This is yet another miraculous move of God. As James and I entered the hospital room where she laid, we met many of her teacher colleagues, friends and family members. There again, the Holy Spirit said to me to lie across her body. I silently said, "Not again Lord." I quietly questioned God, 'in front of all these people?' Just think for a moment how strange and crazy this action would have looked, but I obeyed the Lord, laid across her body and prayed compassionately in English and in tongues.

It didn't matter how awkward it was, she was miraculously healed. The following morning, Sister Janet, her friend called back bright and early, with the good report that the bleeding had ceased that same night. Now being healed, this young lady decided to attend church, and eventually became a member of our congregation. The rest is history. My, my, my! To God be the glory again y'all – His wonders to perform, Hallelujah!

In 2010: I prayed for a sixteen-year girl in Deep Waters, with a unique case of depression. It was a matter of a diabolical origin, and was manifesting itself on her body. She was out of school for a long time. Doctors couldn't help her, but upon request by her mom to pray for her, God intervene after I had prayed for her on a couple of occasions. She, too, was healed and was soon able to go back to school. Today, she is an office professional. Glory, praise, and thanks to Almighty God!

In 2010: One Sunday morning, as I was preaching, the Holy Spirit revealed that a family who migrated to Anguilla from Guyana was about to have their dwelling house repossessed by the bank. While preaching, I was moved to say what the Holy Spirit had told me. Well, at the end of the service, the sister came to me and asked how I knew of her situation in Guyana. She complained that her husband, who was sitting next to her, was nudging her and accused her of telling me of their business. But no, we had never had such a conversation.

That Sunday evening, she came to our home and freely explained their circumstances. To make a long story short, God intervene and saved their house. God is everywhere looking out for His own, Hallelujah!

In 2011: While in Sunday School, one Sunday morning, I heard a loud rumbling noise close to the church. It seemed like it was coming down The

Valley Road in the area of the Post Office. I rushed outside on the porch just to see where the noise was coming from, but I could not tell, so I returned inside. Again, to me, the noise became permeable and louder. I was amazed that no one else but me heard it. Being so restless, again I rushed outside to see if I could detect the source of the rumbling noise. I was troubled in my spirit. It was then the Holy Spirit informed me that there was to be a catastrophic happening in a distance land. I told one particular sister that something is happening afar off. Well, it was a few days later that we learnt of the earthquake and tsunami in Japan.

That 2011 earthquake and tsunami, called the Tōhoku earthquake and tsunami, was the most powerful ever recorded in Japan, and the fourth most powerful earthquake in the world. By all accounts, almost 20,000 lives were lost and 6,200 people were injured.

I am still amazed that God gave me a revelation of the tragic incident, in distant land, before it actually occurred.

In 2011: Our church learned that a certain dancehall artist was scheduled to perform in Anguilla. He had been banned from entering certain countries in the region because of his immoral behavior on stage and the vulgar lyrical contents of his songs. We realized that this artist was having a bad influence on our young people. Well, the No-Walls Church took up the mandate to go before God to intervene in prayer.

We prayed that God would not to allow this artist on the shores of Anguilla. It was a Sunday night that we gathered on the grounds of the General Post Office, next to the area in the Herbert's Complex where a pre-show event was being held to welcome the popular dancehall icon. That night, we prayed fervently, hard and long. The following day we learned that the artist was jailed for a crime that he allegedly committed. Our prayers had been answered and, of course, the show was cancelled. God is worthy, worthy to be praised.

In 2011: I was requested to pray for Sister Janet's mother, who lives In Guyana and was suffering from a condition in one of her eyes. I prophesied that it was her left eye that was affected, and so it was. As I prayed, God miraculously healed her eye. A few days later, she called Sister Janet with the good news of God's healing power. Thanks and praise to Jehovah God!

In 2012: I prayed for Pastor Jim Richardson, who had laid in the Princess Alexandra Hospital suffering for several weeks. The Holy Spirit had arrested me one night as I slept. I was awakened with a devastating stomachache. The Holy Spirit then brought Pastor Jim to my mind.

As an intercessor, I prayed for his healing that night. In the morning, I went to the hospital, laid hands on his stomach. His ailment was in the same area where I was feeling pain the night before. I prayed for him and also declared a prophetic word to his family relative to the Church that he pastored. I assured the family that he was going to be well, and God will rise him up to continue being the Shepherd of his flock.

Pastor Jim was miraculously healed. During the service when I was commissioned as a Prophetess, he gave his testimony, praising and thanking God for another lease on life. The rest is history, but the man of God lives to tell of the goodness and greatness of the Lord. Truly, we serve an awesome God!

In 2012: One night, I was awakened from sleep with irregular heartbeat. The Holy Spirit quickened my spirit to pray for my brother, Lester, who resides in the US. So I prayed to God to send His ministering angels to keep charge over him and to heal him. The next morning, I received a call from my sister, Joyce, who told me that they had to rush him to the emergency room that same night with a heart attack. Our brother was miraculously healed. God be praised for His healing power!

In 2012: One Sunday morning, as service was in session, a well-known teacher, Teacher Debbie, came to the service with her daughter, who was suffering from an unusual ailment. She was unable to walk on her own. She had to be assisted into the church building during a worship session. As I led worship, I paused and asked the mother to bring her to the front of the church.

After prayers were offered up, I held the young lady around her waist. I lifted her to her feet and I began to slowly walk around in the sanctuary with her. As we walked, and while I glorified the Lord, the healing power of the Holy Spirit was infused within her body. The young lady was becoming stronger and stronger, as her feet were gaining strength. Suddenly, she was able to run around the church all by herself.

She was gloriously and miraculously healed! The church was enraptured in a frenzy of praises and worship unto God, as some folks themselves began running, praising and thanking God. The next week, it was reported that the young lady went back out to work, wearing her high heel shoes. To God be the glory, great acts He has done.

In 2012: One morning, while I was in my office a young lady, Michelle Green, called me in distress. She was crying profusely because her younger sister in Jamaica had gone missing. She mentioned that she had an older sister who was abducted the previous year and was killed. She was missing for several days before her body was found dead. She had been kidnapped, raped, killed and left in the bushes. This case was broadcasted on local news media in Jamaica.

Now this distraught young lady feared for her younger sister's life as well. She feared she would succumb to the same fate. This was only one year after the other sister was killed.

I, immediately went into a vibrant prayer over the phone. I fervently beseeched God on the family's behalf, when I heard the Holy Spirit emphatically say to me: "Tell her that God has intervened and that her sister is going to be Ok." With that, I consoled her and assured her that God had saved the life of her sister, and that she was going to be alright.

Well, later that evening, she got word from her family in Jamaica that her sister was found in an abandon building, raped and battered, but she was alive. God faithfully came through for this young lady and her family.

The following Sunday, she came to the Church and gave her testimony of what God had done. Such a merciful and loving Father we serve. Blessed be the Holy name of Jesus!

In 2012: The No-Walls Church had moved to its new location in the Farrington. It was almost a year prior to this, that Holy Spirit in a vision showed me a peculiar rainbow. On a table, in the sanctuary, I got the unction to display the colors of the rainbow using hand towels. Members of the church and visitors would recall that table, in one corner, decked with colorful hand towels.

Well, it was not until two years later, in 2014, that I was inspired to write in my booklet, "Rainbows: God's Covenant with Anguilla", what God was saying about His promises to us as a nation. That year, rainbows were evident all across the island. Some days, they would show up intermittently from sunrise to sun down. We saw single rainbows, double rainbows, in the east, west, north and south. There were rainbows that appeared to be so close, you could almost reach out and touch them. So phenomenal; so glorious! I say glory to God for His marvelous creation.

In 2012: One Saturday afternoon, while the youth leader was engaged with her dancers in a rehearsal session, for a Sunday morning presentation, I sat at the back of the church looking at them and was relishing the moment. Suddenly, the Holy Spirit revealed to me that the youth leader was pregnant, and that she didn't know it.

I waited until rehearsal was over and simply told her what the Spirit revealed to me, that she was pregnant. She responded with a kind of look that I will never forget. I felt rather bad for telling her what the Spirit had said. She appeared to be offended. A couple weeks later, she confirmed that indeed she was pregnant and asked that I be one of the God-parents for the child. Oh my Lord! Again, I say to God be the glory.

In 2012: I prophesied to my son Patville's girlfriend, as I greeted her one Sunday after church, and told her that she was three months pregnant. Indeed, she was pregnant with our first grandson. Well, the next day Patville questioned me, asking how I knew she was three months pregnant. I said to him that only God could have revealed it to me. To God be, all the glory and the honor.

In 2012: I prayed for a well-known tailor who lived in The Quarter. He was so sick that he eventually decided to go to England for medical attention. While there in the hospital, his situation grew worse. A priest was called in to pronounce his last rites. Well, James got information of this and decided to contact him. We prayed fervently to God, with him over the phone, that he would be healed.

God miraculously healed him. Soon he was back in Anguilla. He came to our church, in The Farrington, and gave his testimony. The Sunday morning service was on a spiritual high when he gave his testimony of God's healing power. However, incidentally, we learnt that he died after a couple years later in his native island, Trinidad.

In 2012: One evening, at our church's new location in The Farrington, we prayed for a young lady who had visited a series of special evangelistic services held on the Blowing Point Ball-field area. This young lady expressed the need for prayers, as she was experiencing some level of supernatural, spiritual torment. Well, she was encouraged to come to the No-Walls Church for prayer, accompanied by the visiting minister who was guest preacher at the Blowing Point services.

As we began ministering to her and praying for her, the atmosphere took a turn in the wrong direction. I soon realized that she was under the influence of demonic powers.

As I continued praying, she started uttering strange words, and demons' voices were heard speaking through her. They were saying that they were not listening to me and that they were not coming out. With their "declaration", she covered her ears – as sign of rebellion to our prayers.

I was totally dependent on the Holy Spirit to do His work, and I knew that He would empower me as I confronted the evil forces within her. I realize it was a task to cast out these devils, and I needed God's supernatural power.

It took a while, for the demons were stubborn not wanting to leave. I continued rebuking and casting out many of the evil elements within her. She began to yoke and spat out a strange looking substance. It was amazing, over time, to see how the Holy Spirit came through and brought us the victory.

She eventually fell to the ground, unconscious and exhausted, after putting up some resistance. She then became calm and regained her composure. Suddenly, she got up from the floor with tears running down her face, giving thanks to Jesus for delivering her. Thank God she was in her right mind, once again.

Oh Lord! We give Glory and Honor to Almighty God for her deliverance. Hallelujah! Isn't God great? Oh yes, He is!

By the way, on the spur of that moment of her spiritual deliverance, it brought back memories of a deliverance service that was held by Evangelist R.W. Shambach in Warner Park, Basseterre, on my native island of St. Kitts. It was in the mid-1970s and I had just turned eighteen. Many churches and their congregations all across St. Kitts were in attendance at these services nightly.

I am led here to comment on the ministry of Bro. Shambach for just a few paragraphs:

R.W. Shambach was an American preacher who dwelt and operated under the anointing of the Holy Spirit, and ministered around the world. He preached the gospel with emphasis on healing for the sick and deliverance for the oppressed, and multiple thousands of persons were set free under his charismatic ministry.

Based in the city of Tyler in Texas, Bro. Shambach's ministry reached far and wide through his radio and TV broadcasts, *The Hour of Power.* His radio ministry was one of those that motivated me and bolstered my faith in Christ during my youthful years.

During his visit to St. Kitts, in his services at Warner Park, Brother Shambach would be praying and casting out demons from one individual, for example, and as soon as he would cast out those demon(s) from one person, simultaneously, demons from other persons would start manifesting at the same time. Other individuals, one by one, would show symptoms of being possessed. This scenario would be repeated over and over throughout a night's service.

These manifestations would be revealed every night, until every possessed man, woman, boy and girl was delivered from their tormenting spirits. One by one, persons would be set free as they were brought by local ministers to the altar for divine deliverance.

I learned that an entire school of deaf and blind children was delivered miraculously as Brother Shambach prayed for them in one of the night's services. Healing was flowing, and God was favoring his people with his power of restoration in an amazing fashion.

It was phenomenal every night to see the power of God at work. During these services, before Brother Shambach prayed for the people who were bound and held captive by evil spirits, he would literally warn Christians all over the park to ensure that they are covered by the blood. He remarked that it was a possibility for the demons which were cast out of persons to take up residence in those who were not secured by the blood of Jesus. It was quite frightening for many who were somewhat uncertain about their faith, but for those who were faithful, it was exciting to see the mighty power of God at work.

By the way, while driving to and from these services on the bus, we, church members, would be singing spirited songs, ensuring we were covered by the blood of Jesus. We were making sure that we would not be host for any of those demons that would be expelled from possessed people.

Wow! Who, but God, could have prepared me for the moment of my deliverance ministry in dealing with the ordeal of liberating this possessed young lady? Thank God for His empowering enablement, the mission of her deliverance was accomplished.

If you are a child of God, if you have been born again by being washed in the blood of Jesus, bear in mind that this is no time to play church. Somewhere along the line, you will be faced with spiritual dilemmas. Uncertainty and doubt will attack your faith. You must be prepared to be used of God to deliver the oppressed, once you are in a position to do so.

I remembered one Sunday night I went to a particular church. As I was parking up, I noticed a commotion going on. People were running out of the church building. When I got closer, I realized what was going on. A young lady was beating up on those in the congregation, and they began running out of the church service.   Upon entering the building, I interceded with God. As I prayed, the Holy Spirit came upon me. I restrained the lady, and I, along with two other persons took her to the altar and prayed for her. Later, one of her family members came and took her home.

As I inquired above, what are you going to do when you are faced with such dilemmas? Will you be prepared to deal with such situations should they arise? And believe me! They will arise, be it in your life, a family member's life, at home, in school, in church, in the neighborhood and or in the community. May God help us to be equipped with the Holy Ghost to confront the inevitable.

Remember, Just as God is at work, the devil is also at work and evil is on the rise. The devil is working overtime. He is empowering *his people* to perform evil agenda. Satan knows that his time is short and his diabolical work must soon come to an end.

In 2013: There was a young lady in her prime, who got involved in a serious motor vehicle accident on a vacant road in The Farrington, late at night, while she was heading home. She was thrown from her car and into a thicket of bushes, in the darkness of night. Fortunately, a lone passerby heard her groans and followed them to find her traumatized and suffering in a terrible state. He raised an alarm in the community, and she was rescued and taken to the hospital.

However, this accident had caused her to suffer much emotional trauma for a couple of years. She was unable to sleep, was depressed, and seemed not to be getting any better. So great was her plight, that her mother decided to bring her to the No-Walls Church of Hope one evening for prayer.

I laid hands on her head, and compassionately prayed to God for her healing. My prayers were fervent and my pleading and petitions were sincere, for I really wanted to see God come through for this brilliant young lady. Her faithful mother was sanctioning my petitions as I beseeched God on their behalf.

Thankfully, she was miraculously healed, and today she is doing very well and is back to being her normal self. She now holds down a significant job in one of Government's prominent offices in Anguilla.

All praise and honor be unto our great Father who knows what's best for His children. Only God is worthy of all our praises.

In 2014: I received the inspiration from the Holy Spirit to write the booklet *"The 'Rainbow': God's Covenant with Anguilla"*. This was a follow up from my **2012 vision** experience, mentioned earlier. The prophecy was fulfilled, depicting rainbows all across the island of Anguilla. I was led to write a letter and send copies of the booklet *"The 'Rainbow': God's Covenant with Anguilla"* to many churches and business places in order to relay what God was saying, especially to the churches. However, several churches rejected the letter and booklet and I was met with staunch criticism. The proprietor of one prominent business entity said to me, "Nobody wants to hear about *no* rainbows."

Well, God is in control and he is still performing His work in this nation of Anguilla. As Sinach sings, He is a way-maker, a promise keeper, and even when we are not seeing it or feeling it, he's still working, He never stops working.

In 2015: My son, Patmore, and I were watching *American Ninja Warriors* one night at about 11:00. The Holy Spirit arrested me to go pray for my son, Patison, in England. With that, I told Patmore to turn off the TV, and I went aside to pray for my son. The following day, Patison called and told us that

123

he had finished work late that night and had missed the train.

Consequently, he had to wait for another train which arrived around 2 o'clock in the morning. While he was waiting alone, he said that four guys came up to him with knives and demanded money. The ordeal could have gone so wrong, but God looks out for His children. Thank God he was spared from harm, particularly by a mother's prayer. Folks, it's all about God and Him alone.

In 2017: I was at my ministry, *"No-Walls Prophetic Worship Healing Ministry"*, in Stoney Ground, on September 3rd. We prayed and repented on behalf of Anguilla, asking God to lessen the impact of the pending Hurricane Irma, which was approaching the island, and would make landfall on September 6th. I prayed that God would spare our lives. I remained still praying at the end of the service while others left for home, leaving the keyboardist, Brother Leroy John, and me alone there.

I could see he was worried with a scary look on his face. I told him that he could leave if he wanted to, but he stayed committed and played many soothing songs to charge the atmosphere while I continued in prayer. The Holy Spirit was inspiring him with songs that petitioned God's mercy, seeing that we were being faced with the brunt of the dreadful hurricane. God heard and answered our prayers as well as the prayers of others. Thanks to a merciful and loving God, though massive storm struck Anguilla head-on, all lives on the island were spared except for one.

In 2018: A few months after Hurricane Irma, I told Pastor Jim Richardson and his wife that I was sensing in my spirit that we were going to be faced with a disease that would change lives. Thereafter, I was inspired by the Holy Spirit to ask an official of the Health Authority if the Ministry of Health was prepared to deal with an epidemic should one break out in Anguilla. She responded by saying that I needed to inquire from the head officials of the Health Authority, for myself.

I did not pursue any further inquiry or made any other comment until the Covid-19 Pandemic emerged. At that time, I called that same officer and asked if she recalled our conversation regarding my mention of a pending epidemic, which actually turned out to be a global pandemic known as Covid-19.

She acknowledged that she vaguely remembered the conversation and sarcastically asked, "Are you taking precaution?" Well, again, the rest is history.

Covid-19 came and disrupted life as we knew it. It was a global catastrophe that took the lives of millions worldwide. Thanks to God, He was merciful enough to spare us again, with only a small minority in the local death toll. I must say thanks, as well, to the Health Authority of Anguillla, and the wisdom of the Government who closed our borders early to avert major loss of life.

In 2018: I prayed for my Mom who resides in the US. She had suffered a heart attack and had almost died. The family called me and said that I needed to come to Connecticut right away, as they feared she was not going to make it. At that time, I had just started a new job at the Manoah Hotel, and was on a three months' probation. I didn't want to lose the job, as there were other persons in line for the position. If I had left before the probation period ended, I might not have retained the job upon my return.

So, I went into warfare prayer, beseeching God to heal Mom and to keep her alive. That afternoon, after work, I sat at home on the back porch and prayed. As I finished praying, suddenly pods from a shady tree flew on the porch like rain, and set before me where I was sitting.

It was as if God was saying I heard you and have answered your prayers. My mom was healed. After passing the three-month probation period, I requested time off to visit her in April, 2018.

However, four years later, June 2022, I was able to travel with my grandson, Jai to visit her and to attend my sister's wedding. Mom was able to attend the wedding too, on July 4th, even though she was confined to a wheel chair. She, none-the-less, enjoyed herself.

The following month, she passed away in August 2022, at the age of 87 years. To God be the glory for the things He hath done in her life!

In 2018: I was awakened by the Holy Spirit with a message from the Lord for the Churches, Ministers of Government and the nation of Anguilla in general. There was a need to get back under the covenant with God, as many had gone after strange gods. I was shown that many persons were involving themselves in witchcraft. With that, I was led to give ear to what the Lord was saying. I was inspired to call DJ Hammer of Klass FM radio, and requested permission to use the radio station to reveal what 'thus saith the Lord'. Without hesitation he consented. The next morning, at about 9:30, I went to the station and delivered the message from the Lord, and left.

Amazingly, a few minutes later, God gave His approval, when, all of a sudden it started raining, lightning and thundering. The weather had suddenly changed, and the inclement conditions persisted into the next evening – a twenty-four hour period. I received calls from many persons who were expressing concern regarding the message I delivered on the radio station that day.

Folks, God is still on His throne and He is looking down on His people. Make no mistake about it. He's to be feared and revered. When we, the church, the Government, Anguilla, and the world at large embrace evil and give a deaf ear and a blind eye to degrading immorality, we are setting up ourselves for swift judgment. God will repay persons for acts of immorality and unrighteous living. Yes, it will come right back, and it will come in unthinkable ways and patterns.

God is no respecter of any man, nation, or, in particular, any church. Many of us are aware of judgments handed down swiftly on some bible characters, like Ananias and Sapphira, King Nebuchadnezzar, and King Herod. The time and season is upon us when the judgment of God will begin at the House of God, according to 1 Peter 4:17, if we continue living unrighteous before Him. We must respect the life of righteousness to which he has called us, for it is a fearful thing to fall into His angry hands.

In 2018: My son and I went into the battle of our lives in court with our landlord to keep a roof over our heads. We had been occupying the house that we now have under a leasehold arrangement. We had entered a special mortgage agreement in August of 2013, but the enemy was fierce enough and hell-bent to regain the property.

Well, I had never been put to such a test in all of my life like I had been tested back then, having to deal with this situation. I was determined that this was a mountain that had to be removed, fiercely, in Jesus' name. I went into tactful warfare prayers, fasting like never before. I had never prayed and fasted like this in my lifetime, and I hope I would not have the need to engage like this again anytime soon.

There were times I fell beneath the load. I buckled helplessly, but morning, noon and night I would go before God in prayer. Sometimes I felt like I would die from not having regular meals – all alone, trusting God to give me strength and the ultimate victory. Oh! But with much tears of joys, my morning came. God came through for us in early 2021.

There were times when the song, *"You Know My Name"*, by Tasha Cobbs, assured me that my God was near and was fighting my battle. This song gave me wings to keep hope alive and to keep me trusting in God.

I had travailed a full three long years, laboring in much prayer for this basic need – a house to dwell in. Also, thanks to the skills of a helpful, God-fearing lawyer, who knows the Lord, I gained the hope that he would fight for our success in the matter in court.

Occasionally, it appeared as if this young man knew our hearts, and though I was not able to utter the right words of explanation, he knew exactly what was on my mind. He had the right attitude and the right intention to deliver what God had called him to do. After three years of relentless fighting and hard work, this well-trained expert lawyer stood the test of time with us. He went above and beyond his call of duty to bring us the victory. I deem this young lawyer to be a special professional who has the heart to help individuals who are being taken advantage of.

All glory goes to God who said in his word, that there is nothing that is too hard for Him to do. He promises that when that old devil, the enemy, comes in like a flood, He, God Himself, will rise up a standard against him. Friends, that is the promise of God I relied on. Let God arise and the enemy be scattered. All glory and honor be to our Almighty God!

Also, in my passage through this ordeal, on May 18, 2019, while watching the show "*The Voice*", the still small voice of the Holy Spirit prompted me to go and close down the living room windows, as accustom every night at a certain time. The show was so interesting that I ignored the voice of the Lord twice. But upon His third warning, His voice was so forceful and permeable in my inner being that I jumped up off the bed and rushed to the living room.

As I was about to pull down the window, I saw the image of a person I know, outside in a suspicious way. I shouted out the person's name and she dodged and ran between some scaffolding, scampered behind the building, and disappeared.

Well, I only realized the damage that was done a few days later. What was done could have been to the detriment to my family and I, but thanks be to God, that weapon formed against us did not prosper. God was protecting us, so no harm could befall us.

I tell you; we are living in a wicked world and the hearts of men and women are involved in gross darkness. To this day, every now and then, strange things would manifest itself in the environment. But let's be prepared to be obedient to the voice of God. Let's pray for our continued safety and protection against these evil days in which we are living.

The hearts of men are becoming desperately wicked, and only God can give protection from the cunning, crafty onslaughts of the enemy.

The sustenance and preservation of our lives must be dependent upon God and God alone. In these last days, when evil will become the norm, in these days when men's hearts will become cold and insensitive, witchcraft will increase and unrighteous living will permeate even the lives of persons who profess to be godly – if we are not under God's covering.

The Bible says that the enemy's job is to steal, kill and destroy. We must become sensitive to our surroundings – our neighborhood and communities. We must get to know how Satan, that old adversary, operates. We must not take things for granted anymore, but become bold and brave enough to expose the enemy and his evil deeds.

In 2020: During the Covid-19 period, I learned from a coworker, that a former boss had become sick with Covid and was not expected to make it. Upon hearing that, I tried reaching out to her, through certain channels, but to no avail. At last, one day I received a call from her, as she related to me the experience she had with Covid. I responded by telling her that I went into prayer and fasting to God for her healing, upon hearing of her plight.

It was quite amazing and strange to hear the way she responded. She said to me, "Patricia, thanks to you and your God". I laughed a bit to myself, but I knew that she was grateful to be alive and I was even the more happy and grateful to God for answering my prayers. He is no respecter of persons, whether a person acknowledges him or not. He would have mercy on whomever He would. I gave my God praise and adoration on her behalf. He is the God of all mankind.

In 2021: My oldest son, Patmore, (a police officer) was engaged on the job with two other officers on an assignment, when he himself was caught up in harm's way. That evening, again I was watching the popular TV show, *"The Voice"*. The Holy Spirit summoned me to go and pray for my son. Right there and then, I knew in my spirit which one of my three sons were in trouble, so I turned off the TV and fervently prayed for him that God would shield and protect him from harm.

I then went back and continue watching the show. Well, it was early the next morning that Patmore knocked on my bedroom door. I told him to open, as I was still in bed. When he opened the door, I was surprised to see a big white patch on his right eye. I was not in the state of shock, but all I asked him: "Did this happened around 10:00, or there about, last night?" he answered, "Yes Mommy". After composing my thoughts, I was able to tell him how the Holy Spirit arrested me to pray for him. He could have lost his right eye.

He said, as he was walking towards a dark abandoned building, he was about to put his phone light on, when he walked right into a rod of steel protruding from a wall of the building. It caught him on the upper portion of the right cheek bone which forms the eye socket. Of course, they had to abort the mission which they were on and his colleagues rushed him to the hospital. Indeed, I give God due thanks and praise for protecting my son. All glory and honor belongs to my Almighty God!

In 2022: While in the U.S. visiting with my sister, one morning she was frantically shouting, calling me. She exclaimed that she had to rush to the emergency room with her son who had suddenly taken ill. With that, my grandson and I ran downstairs to the basement where her son resides. I observed that my nephew was in a really bad state. We sped off with him in her SUV.

When we got to the hospital, my sister's fiancé and I were not allowed to enter the emergency room with her, due to Covid-19 restrictions. So, on the spur of the moment, I beckoned to her as she was heading towards the elevator with her son in a wheel chair, "Let me pray for him," I said to her. I went into an urgent session, making supplications to a merciful God. As soon as I finished praying for him, he released a big belch or burp.

I knew right there and then that he was healed, and that he would be OK. We later learned he was diagnosed with kidney infection, according to his Mom.   Before we know it, he was released and was able to walk his mother, along with his brother, down the aisle on her wedding day, July 4th, 2022.

In 2022: In November, I was lying in bed watching the U.S. Mid-term Election results, when all of a sudden, I was moved to pray for my son Patison in the UK again. After praying, I made it a point to call my other son, Patville, to inquire how they were doing. I wanted to especially find out how Patison was keeping as it was him whom I was prompted to pray for. Besides, it was usually easier to contact Patville than to reach Patison.

Patville sought to assure me that they were doing fine. However, when I called him the following morning, he reported that Patison had gone to the hospital for attention. He was experiencing severe back pains. Obedient to the Spirit's bidding, I had already prayed proactive prayers, sent up to the heart of God on my son's behalf, the evening before. I thank God for answering my prayers. Patison recovered speedily, and God is to be praised.

2023: My ten-year old grandson, Jai, is quite sensitive and appreciative of the goodness of God, and he was eager for me to "drop" his experience of how God healed him. He said, "Na-Na, it would only make sense to tell what God did for me". So, here is his account of his healing, even as it is the final, in this series of testimonials.

Recently, Jai contracted a severe cold with a "roasting fever". It was the second week after school had reopened, following the Christmas holidays. His case became worse during the earlier part of the evening. I became quite worried. I tried every possible home remedy, making up concoctions which I thought would bring about relief. But instead, his condition grew worse, and I was at my whit's end. He was in much pain and discomfort, and he was talking "out of his head" unintelligently.

I was tempted to take him to the hospital, as the spirit of fear and worry came over me. As I contemplated taking him to the hospital, the Holy Spirit momentarily arrested my conscience. He said "Come on, pray for the child!" It was about 12:30-1:00 am, or there about. I suddenly became so convicted for being fearful and about worrying, that I had forgotten to pray at first.

I asked God's forgiveness in repentance. With that, I held my grandson's limp body in my arms like a little biddy baby and I uttered a mighty, compassionate prayer with tears streaming down my face. I was crying out to the Master of this storm, rebuking the fever and asking God to speak a "Peace be still" to the situation.

Instantly, the fever diminished. Jai became as quiet as a lamb and went straight to sleep and woke up around 5:00 am, in the morning, as "good as gold". He went on his iPad and was playing games, as if nothing had happened. Jai was healed, thanks to a loving, faithful and a forgiving God!

My goodness, what an ordeal that was for me, I was so helpless, I forgot to call on the Master initially. Here I was, trying out all forms of home remedies, wrapping him with heated Sour Sop leaves, gave him Nyquil, rubbing him with Vaporize rub and using ice, trying to break the fever, etc. etc., before been convicted by the Holy spirit that I should pray....

God will never give up on us, nor give us more than we can bear, even in our lowest and weakest moments. I can laugh at that situation now. We are free to have a sense of humor with God. And though I felt really bad when Holy Spirit convicted me, I am so glad that He did. Oh! Hallelujah!

The song: "If you try everything and everything failed, try Jesus", came to mind, right out of the blue. It was a lesson well learned. I am determined now, more than ever, to put Jesus first in everything I do. And I would like to encourage others to do the same and watch Him work on their behalf, Amen!

Many other instances of healing, deliverance and prophetic unction were wrought by God's hands via the Ministry that God gave me. However, I think the foregone accounts are enough to provide sufficient inspiration and to encourage the reader to trust in God. He will provide protection, healing, deliverance and preservation for the sustenance of life in general.

I pray that as you read this book, and especially if you or someone you know is in need of healing and deliverance from any oppressive situation, that the Spirit of God will quicken your faith, mind and spirit, to supernaturally bring about healing for you and your acquaintances – right now! Be heal in the name of Jesus, God has the power to set you free from whatever aliment that may affect your being. Rise up and walk in victory! Amen.

While the subject here concerns healing and deliverance from sicknesses and oppression, I am led to sound a particular alarm. Please observe the note below, which concerns persons getting sick after taking the Lord's sacrament, or communion.

A Note on Being Sick:

When it comes down to being sick, I have a profound word of advice for Christians. I have noticed lately that there are many church folks who partake of the sacrament, the Eucharist, or communion, as it is called, that not long after partaking of it, it is reported that some individuals, here and there, become sick.

Well, just in case you may not realize it, partaking of the sacrament is a very serious, solemn act in God's sight. Let us be real about it. The sacrament is not merely for the display of some religious order.

God the Father presented Christ His son, offering Him up as an innocent sacrificial Lamb for sins of every kind. This Lamb, Jesus Christ, was free of guilt – and free of sin. When we take part in the act of the sacrament, or communion, we are participating in an act which commemorates the pure and holy sacrifice of Christ. We are joining ourselves together with Him – in "communion".

In essence, we are identifying with the broken body of Jesus through eating the bread and we are identifying with his shed blood by the drinking of the wine.

We need to bear in mind that Christ's body and His life, when it was sacrificed, was innocent, pure and holy – without flaws or spots.

When we, at some point in our lives, initiate his salvation by applying to Him to forgive us of our sins and save us, then He washes us clean by that precious blood which was shed in sacrifice. Once we are clean, we must seek to maintain this cleanliness by living our lives in line with His truth and righteousness. So, how can one so brazenly go and partake of the sacrament when there is sin in his or her life?

Well, think about it: This is the only direct reason for the cause of sickness and death, pointed out in the scriptures:

Let us listen to what the Apostle Paul says in 1 Corinthians 11: 27-29: *"Therefore whoever eats this bread or drinks this cup of the Lord in an unworthy manner will be guilty of the body and blood of the Lord. But let a man examine himself, and so let him eat of the bread and drink of the cup. For he who eats and drinks in an unworthy manner eats and drinks judgment to himself, not discerning the Lord's body."* Then, 1 Corinthians 11: 30, says, *for this reason many are weak and sick among you, and many sleep (die)."*

Wow! Do we understand the serious implications of eating Jesus' body and drinking His blood when we harbor sin in our life? God makes no excuses. And He makes no exceptions. One must first sincerely examine his or her life, and the heart must first be cleansed prior to partaking of the "holy sacrament". We should not treat the sacrament so lightly or be willy-nilly about it. It is serious, my friend.

Paul announces, through the Holy Spirit's inspiration, God's judgment under His authority. He says: this is the reason why some people get sick and it is for this reason why they die. Let us be aware of the manner in which we partake of God's body and drinking of His blood.

Chapter 14:

"Twenty-Twenties and Beyond"

I sense that it is going to be a period of judgment and reward for the decisions and choices we make, whether good or bad. God is going to reward "good" choices with blessings and "bad" decisions with His wrath – which will be handed down through certain consequences in our lives.

The devil will continue to steal, kill and destroy more people in 2023 and beyond. Death will increase more and more in this darkened world globally. But hear this, people of God – and I am referring to true Christians, now:

God will make sure that His elect ones are provided for and that they are protected and covered in hard times. But we must make sure we are sensitive to the Spirit of God to ensure the blood is over our door post and our house is in order.

Now is time to make the choice, whether you're going to stay in the devil's territory and suffer God's wrath, or pay your allegiance to God and enjoy his bountiful blessings. To be on the fence with a mindset of indecision is also dangerous. Why halt between two opinions? You are either on the Lord's side or on the side of the adversary. So, are you going to get off the fence and get on "this train" to Glory in order to reap God's reward of eternal life?

Revelation 22:11 points out a clear distinction of the condition of man's heart in these end times. Hear what the Spirit said through John the Revelator: *"He who is unjust, let him be unjust still; he who is filthy, let him be filthy still; he who is righteous, let him be righteous still, and he who is holy, let him be holy still."* The choice is yours in these end times, my friend.

I have a word for "Worshippers, Prayer Worriers and Intercessors": Now is the time to arm ourselves with the anointing. Most of the time, we only talk of the presence of God, but what about the anointing of God? It is the Spirit's anointing that breaks yokes and bondages from us and the people that are around us – those people whom we may be asked to pray for. In such cases, we need to pray with the anointing. One must be anointed to change and shift an atmosphere, in our prayer meetings and worship services.

We sing certain songs with fine titles but the anointing is not there to affect the change of what we are singing about. Sure, the singing was good enough for a shout, a dance and a good feeling, but not anointed enough to the extent that it would create or bring change beyond our emotions.

It was Jesus, Himself, who claimed in Luke 4:18: *"The Spirit of the Lord God is upon me, and he has anointed me to preach good tidings unto the meek; he hath sent me to bind up the brokenhearted, to proclaim, liberty to the captives, and the opening of the prison to them that are bound."* Yes, in order to do God's work on earth, one must be empowered with **the anointing**.

The presence of God is everywhere. And while many people liken His presence to "goose bumps", He is spiritually tangible and it is much more than just goose bumps. Wherever God's presence is, there is liberty to perform and to do His work. His work can be only done through us, his vessels, who are **anointed** and set aside for His use.

It is through the **anointing** that chains of oppression and depression are broken; it is through the **anointing** that sicknesses are cured, people are healed, and captive souls are delivered and freed.

Coupled with the **anointing**, we also need the Spirit of discernment to see and know, in the Spirit realm, the works of the devil in churches, in our schools, our homes and our communities. The *anointing* of the Spirit is really the game changer. Oh how we need the *anointing* like never before!

Steer Clear of Vulgar Rhythms

I have a word for Worshippers, Intercessors, Prayer Warriors and all of God's people everywhere, I say arise and put on your garments of prayer, praise, and worship. Praise and worship the God of your salvation. I call upon worshippers, particularly, to begin playing worship songs in your homes, in your neighborhoods, and in your surroundings. Let your environment be charged with an atmosphere of worship. Our world is infested with too many vulgar and fleshly man-made "songs" that are being filtered via technological media.

These vulgar, ruthless rhythms permeate the airwaves and cause the atmosphere to change from God's natural glorious state to the spiritual darkness of the devil. *Righteousness is on the decline.* The shield of righteousness that once covered God's people is deteriorating, much as the natural ozone layer that shielded the earth is being eaten away.

Ministers of God, we need to saturate ourselves with *anointed* worship music. Let it be our lifestyle.

By doing so, you will be sure to find out where the enemy is hiding; you will notice that friends and neighbors will be agitated if they are agents of the enemy, Satan. Do not play your worship music too loud to disturb the peace, as some people just might be bothered by it.

Just know that the devil and his agents are not able to tolerate or stand the things of God. Worship and music are God's pleasure, and the man or woman with a carnal mind cannot stand to hear it. Their tolerance level to the things of God is zero-rated. Some neighbors may complain, or leave the area, and might even close their doors and windows so that they are not bothered by your worship.

As we are witnessing changes in our world, we must change also, but for the better. We must allow our spirituality to rise up in God for the good. God does not change; we change, and sometimes we change for the worst. We sometimes begin to second guess who and whose we are and become adoptable to the change all around us, as we endeavor to mimic the styles of the secular. Some people have compromised their convictions to adapt to changes around them by way of music, a culture, new technology, church affiliated doctrines and beliefs that run counter to godliness.

What is so strange is that when the world blasts its vulgar sounding nuisance, which they call "music", we, the children of God, say nothing. However, we are responsible to God to change the atmosphere for the good, and as the spiritually violent ones, let us take the atmosphere by force for the glory of God.

There is a secret to playing genuine worship music: It helps to keep the devil away from your surroundings. Satan hates worship. I mean true worship. Also, watch and see, the rain will start to fall and the heat will subside. The atmosphere will change. Can you image the outcome if worshipers everywhere, in every corner of the globe, spend time playing sacred songs and listening to wonderful worship music?

Let's join in with Cee Cee Winans and sing: "Yes the world will bow down and say you are God, every man will bow down and say you are King; So let's start right now, why would, we wait? King of Glory fill this place, we just want to be with you."

Christians, let's cover our areas where we live and set about changing our neighborhoods. I am not telling you to do anything that I am not doing myself. I play pure worship music and do worship unto God every day, whenever it is possible. I have gained many spiritual benefits by doing so. My spirit-man stays encouraged and refreshed.

And just in case you become tired of the repetitious radio songs, I would like to introduce you to a YouTube radio station named *"K-Love"*, an American station. One humorous song on this station that inspires and motivates me is a song that says: "The devil wants to kick me out of the church, but you can't take the church out of me."

K-Love features songs to meet your every need. Some of my favorite artists are: Richard Smallwood, Donnie McClurkin and the Gather Vocal Band, among so many others. Richard Smallwood sings a song that I suggest you should listen to. It's a song in which he says: "Thanks for waking me up this morning." I play this song repeatedly and religiously every day. Others like "Hold on Don't Let Go", "He's everything" and "Praises Wait for Thee" are among some of my favorites. These are just awesome songs that would fill your souls with praise and worship unto the Lord.

Remember, when we set ourselves to worship the Lord, He requires us to worship Him in Spirit and in truth. I have observed that there are some church leaders and worshippers who indulge in certain lifestyles of fornication, adultery, lying, stealing and other unrighteous acts, but they are not afraid to go to the House of God and funk it up with "strange worship".

Many Worship Ministers do not give God a "lick of worship" during the week but can't wait for Sunday morning to come. Well, do we not know that worship should be a sincere act of obedience before the Lord daily? It is to be a sweet smelling savor unto the supreme God of the universe. It is to Him that we must eventually give account. So when some worship ministers and leaders live loosely, then go to the House of God to worship, they are, in essence, saying to God, this is what you deserve, dear Lord – from an unclean vessel.

This trait goes all across the board, from the pulpit to the door. Fellow Leaders and Minsters of Worship, when this happens, all we are doing is giving off the aroma of whatever sin(s) characterizes our lifestyle.

If you fornicate, all you are doing is giving off that spirit of fornication and sending up to God a fornicating or adulterous aroma. When that is done, the congregation breathes it in and propagates the same. The church in turn becomes infiltrated with all kinds of spirits, thus causing the "*Body of Christ*" to be spiritually sick and of none effect.

Eventually, the very nation becomes sick too, where all kinds of illnesses and disease and death occur. Besides, vicious crimes like murder that stem from greed, resentment and hatred overtake our societies and plague our nations. Why? Because, we the church is sin-sick, lame, and ineffective.

In many instances, the light of the church is being diminished and hardly has any effect on the nation because we have allowed sin to darken our doors, thus, the "sinner man or woman" cannot even see the light whereby he or she can come in to be saved – like it used to be. I know this message here is a rather harsh note to conclude on, but for the sake of promoting righteousness, I must be a mouth-piece of the Lord.

The scripture ascertains that Satan is the prince of the power of the air, and he manages the spirit that work in the children of disobedience, according to Ephesians 2:2. There are so many vicious things happening around us which he is the author of. There is violence and crime and political unrest;

there is gambling, prostitution, acts of fornication, broken homes and social unrest. Our societies are on the edge of moral decay. But, as the old Caribbean chorus says, "It's amazing what praises can do." So let us sing praises to our Father. His Holy Spirit will make a difference.

I am not telling you to do anything that I am not doing myself. I play pure worship music and do worship unto God on a daily basis. I gain many spiritual benefits by doing so. My spirit-man stays encouraged and refreshed, my mind stays at ease, my stress level is lower, and I allow God to work on my hopes and aspirations for my future.

We are the Church – the called-out ones. We are the *ecclesia*. We must be separated from the world and consecrated to God who has called us from darkness into His marvelous light.

As the *Body of Christ*, we are privileged in Christ, my friends. We are even called to set the tone for Government. In turn, the government would govern through the atmosphere set by the Church. Then, and only then, God's favorable change will come to the nation.

Do you wonder why Government has to grapple in frustration with political and social issues? Do you wonder why Governments are unable to work effectively for the good of the people they are supposed to lead and serve? Take a look at the condition of the Church. And until the Church – God's Ministers and Leaders – change their ways, then Government will not change, and the nation will not see change for good.

So, what are we going to do, Church? May God help us to begin to know who we are and whose we are? I know we have missed the mark over time, and as some people say, the church is not perfect—that is right. The church is by no means perfect right now – not by a long shot. However, this does not mean that we must continue to live the way we do. We need to be mindful that we must strive to be righteous and holy.

When we are spiritually conscious to move in that direction, we are well on our way to becoming *perfect* at the end of the day. We would be conscientiously moving on to that stage of perfection that God requires.

Jesus, the Son of God is our great example. He was tempted just as we are tempted, yet without sin.

As Christians, we must strive to be like Him, patterning our lives from His model. Listen to what He commands us after he had preached His 'Sermon on the Mount'. He said: "Be ye therefore perfect, even as your Father is perfect." Jesus knows that perfection is possible, you see? But it requires a life of sacrifice, just as He made the sacrifice.

You may ask: What kind of sacrifice is required? Well, we are called to relinquish life's immoral pleasures; to give up the sinful acts that appease our fleshly appetites. That is the only way that the Church and Christians, at large, will be respected and regarded as "Christians". Holiness must be 'our watchword and song'.

Perfection comes as a result holy living. Let us hear what the Apostle said about it in 1 Peter 1:16. He commands us: "As it is written, Be ye holy, even as I am holy". Peter was making reference to a major command in the Levitical law, which is indeed still relevant for 21st Century Christians today. In Leviticus 11:45, the Lord God commands: "For I am the Lord, who brought you up out of the land of Egypt to be your God. You shall therefore be holy, for I am holy."

We have no excuse not to become perfect; we have no excuse not to be holy. In His Kingdom Agenda, God is bringing His Church into His perfectness before His Son returns. It is our duty to do our part since we are His Bride, to clad ourselves as the Bride of Christ – the Church of God. God expects His Church to repent, change our ways, and live righteously before Him. Remember what He says in His word: ***"Righteousness exalts a nation, but sin brings reproach upon a people."*** Proverbs 13:3.

Chapter 15:

"A Call to Worship"

Worship is our response to God for who God is and for all that God is to us. We do not worship God for what we can get from Him or for what we can get out of the worship experience.

Worship is not just having a "good time". Instead, our reason for worshipping should be imbedded in the realization that God is sovereign, he is supreme, and there is no other being with characteristics as holy and as divine as His. God Jehovah is the only God, that is worthy of our worship.

Four Characteristics of a true Worshipper, according to John 4: 20-24:

1. The Object of a true worshipper's worship must be God –sovereign God; supreme God.
2. The Attitude of a true worshipper must be the right one. He or she must have the attitude of the Spirit, and he or she must be humble enough to be led – led by the Spirit.
3. The Standard by which a true worshipper is measured must be the Standard of truth – pure, undefiled reality that encompasses the realm of the divine image of the true and living, infallible God.
4. The Lifestyle of a true worshipper must be a life of devotion to God. This lifestyle can be developed by reading God's word, prayer, making melodies in your heart through singing and by being a witness to others.

When a believer aligns himself or herself with these four qualities that are exercised in worship, namely: the Object of worship; the Attitude of worship; the Standard of worship and the Lifestyle of worship, then the worship experience would be a rewarding one. Consequently, God would provide us with the enablement and strength to bear the burdens of life, and He will supply the power to fight against the forces of evil.

Yes, God will give us the confidence and provide deliverance even in the atmosphere of worship, as long as the worshipper's Object, Attitude, Standard and Lifestyle are involved in the worship experience. The worshipper, therefore, can lead a victorious life of total trust in God and of total triumph in Jesus, God's son.

A true worshipper will not be tired of worshipping. Living a life of service and constant worship might lead one to ask: "What is in it for me?" This is a question that a worshipper might be concerned about. God gets the glory, and He is the object of our praise when we worship, but what benefits are there for us as worshippers when we exercise our gifts and talents in worship before the Lord?

One of the prime benefits that a true worshipper should expect is the anointing. God furnishes us with the anointing through the Holy Spirit when we submit ourselves in worship before Him. The Holy

Spirit, therefore, is an extremely important facet of true worship, and the true worshipper should be careful to always invite the presence of the Spirit into the worship experience.

When the Holy Spirit is come, the worshipper will receive the anointing and thus, will be empowered for Christian service. This empowerment is another benefit which the worshipper will gain from worshipping.

It was Jesus Himself who testified: "The Spirit of the Lord is upon me, and He has anointed me..." Let us bear in mind, that it was not only Jesus who had need for the anointing. Hundreds of years before Jesus spoke those words, they were originally spoken by the prophet Isaiah. Isaiah realized that, as a man of God, he needed to be empowered — He stood in need of the power of God.

The only way he could receive this power and anointing is through the Spirit. Thus, he claimed like Jesus did years after: "The Spirit of the Lord is upon me, and He has anointed me." According to Luke 4:18, He has anointed me to preach the gospel to the poor; to heal the brokenhearted; to proclaim liberty to the captives; to give sight to the blind; to set free those who oppressed and to proclaim the acceptable year of the Lord.

Jesus was God son, manifested in flesh upon the earth. Through his virgin birth, as God, He also condescended to human kind. Being human, in order for Him to be empowered, it was necessary that He depend upon the third person in the trinity, the Holy Spirit, to receive His anointing and His empowerment.

Thus, again, we see how essential the Holy Spirit is in our worship experience. Without the Spirit, worship would be a dwarf maze of powerless performance. Again, it was Jesus Himself who said: "You shall receive power *after* the Holy Spirit has come upon you." That is the anointing which Jesus was referring to through the Holy Spirit.

Some people do not catch the revelation of the relationship between the power of the Spirit and the anointing. I wish to emphasize that the Holy Spirit brings the anointing, and in turn, the anointing gives us power. So, what's in the worship experience for you? Well, true worship, worship in Spirit and in truth, will give you power for service through the constant exposure to God's Holy Spirit.

Since God is to be the exclusive object of our worship, then, we are not to worship:

. Departed saints. People's relatives who have died should never be regarded as the recipients of worship. Some people, even Christians, make the mistake of bringing themselves to the place of consciously paying tribute in prayers and petitions to their dead ancestors. But God alone is worthy of worship.

. The devil. Of course, Satan, our adversary, is vying for our worship. He competes with God. He gets jealous, as you know, when all of Christendom, all around the world, pays tribute in worship to Jehovah. So jealous is he that he tried to coax Jesus Himself to bow down and "honor" him in worship, trying to bargain with the Master.

The thing is that we can unconsciously worship the devil without even realizing it. He is the adversary of our souls, and when we worship with the wrong mindset and motive, we please him. In true worship, the focus must be directed to God Himself. If the focus is on one's self, God gets no glory. If the focus is on projecting a prideful image, then God gets no praise. Guess who gets the glory and praise – yes, the devil.

. Angels. Though these are heavenly beings, they should not be worshipped. They   dwell where God is, and they are His messengers, His warriors, the protectors of His saints, etc., but they should never be regarded as the object of our worship. They are simply *created creatures,* and they are not the Creator.

4. <u>The Virgin Mary</u>. Certain religions pay tribute to Mary because she is the mother of Jesus our Savior. However, it is important for such people to realize that though she is Jesus' mother, she is in *no way* God, and must not be worshipped as such. Only God is to be worshipped, not the Virgin Mary of any other created being.

When the angel Gabriel told Joseph that Mary was conceived of the *Holy Ghost,* it meant that God the Father's agent on earth, which is the Holy Spirit, the third person of the God-head, had impregnated Mary. Mary was simply an instrument of God, subject to the working of the Holy Spirit, to bring forth God's Son.

5. <u>Any person or other gods.</u> Of course, we are forbidden not to worship man or any other god or idol. We are forbidden of God not to worship any other creature because only God Jehovah must be recognized as God.

God is the audience of true worship. As we worship God, we must realize that God is "Holy." Thus, we must approach Him in reverence with godly fear. Consider what happens when men encounter the holiness of God. When we worship, we must consider ourselves as nothing. God must increase while we decrease. Let us look at Abraham as he worshipped the Lord.

He confessed that he was *"dust and ashes"*. Similarly, Job said, *"I abhor myself"; and repent in dust and ashes;" and* Habakkuk *"trembled"* in the presence of God.

Ezra, as well, said that he was too ashamed and humiliated to lift up his face before God.
A true worshipper should not approach God in a flippant manner.

Worship time is a time of reverence, because
God is holy, and we must approach Him with awe. God providentially gives us the opportunity to share in His mercy.

A worshiping soul is a grateful and penitent soul.
Worshiping in the Spirit
begins with the life of the worshipper, and the attitude of a true worshipper must be evident long before he or she gets to the House of God.

Worship has a close and intimate relationship
with life, although all of life is not worship. Our conduct, our lifestyle, and attitudes relate to our worship.

It is observed, that at times when genuine worship is taking place and God's glory Is filling the house, the moderator of the service would abruptly halt the fervent worship to give way to the "preaching of the Word".

I have witnessed this trait several times. It causes God to become short changed of the worship He requires.

In most services, the realm of the Shekinah glory of God is not reached because we are too busy with our programs that we are so accustomed to. We fail to notice when the glory comes. It is God's time! We must learn to be sensitive to the spirit of discernment, and to give the Holy Spirit His space in our services.

This is the most important part of our worship.

Remember, God said He is seeking true worshippers; He didn't say He's seeking for a preacher man.

Yes, the Word is important, but when intimate and spirited worship reaches a climax, it changes the atmosphere and provides the opportunity for healings, miracles and other supernatural benefits.

The presence of the Holy Spirit provides the vehicle to soften and water the ground so that the Word is preached effectively.

An anointed session of worship prepares the hearts of men to receive salvation as the altar call is given. In these moments, we must be careful to see the need for culturing the presence of the Holy Spirit.

When this happens, we will achieve all that there is to gain from worship, and God, in turn, will pour out of His supernatural blessings.

We will see revelation, transformation, and salvation are all released by the Holy Ghost in worship sessions like these, once the Spirit is cultured. Such benefits as these are seldom attained when a spirited worship is abruptly aborted to give way to the "message".

While the preacher may be eager to get the sermon across, this should not be done at the expense of forfeiting an anointed worship session. The more we allow the glory of God to linger, the more the anointing will become distinctly evident in our midst.

Subsequently, we will lose all control, and He gains total control of the service. Have you ever heard the phrase: "it's not about you", "It's about God", as one individual tries to put down another? Well, too often, we miss out making it about Him and all about us. Let us change and consider our ways.

Let us become sensitive to the Spirit's leading as we worship. May we today, allow the Holy Spirit of God to take full control of our services.

As we prepare for the return of Jesus Christ, I see true, sincere Worshippers sprinting to the finish line. All of the genuine worshippers may not be in the same rank or position, but we are all moving in the same direction and advancing as the army of God to one final destination and that is Heaven.

Some may be a little slower and a little weaker. Some of us may be battered by the storms of life's affairs. But we will ultimately overcome. "Greater is He that is in you," the scripture says, "than he that is in the world.

I see your vibrant joy. May it give you that strength that you need to fight against discouragement. I see that your faith is intact, and your anchor still holds. So, be courageous and steadfast in hope as you faithfully complete the race.

To reiterate, the spirit of a true worshipper must be linked to a right attitude. What you think about and how you feel as you worship matters.

True worship involves more than just the right externals. We are to offer up spiritual sacrifices as we draw near to God with a *"true heart",* according to Hebrews 10:22. And as Ephesians 5:19 encourages us, we are to: *"Sing and make melody in your hearts Unto the Lord."*

...me things we should not do in order that our ...earts would be ready to Worship in spirit and in uth:

first of all, do not disrespect the sanctuary or place of worship. Do not be bored and indifferent to the worship environment.

do not have a cold, callous unforgiving heart towards a brother or a sister but a heart of kindness, fear and reverence.

do not be bored and indifferent or in a hurry to get over with worship and "get out of there".

do not have your minds on other activities, or be distracted, but be attentive and focused.

do not let your minds stray on any other recipients of your worship, but focus on God, and Him alone.

Four types of worshippers:

The Holy Spirit has revealed to me that there are four types of worshippers. While all four types may be joined by some common thread of faith and paying homage to a god, there are indeed distinguishable differences.

Worshipper A—this is a person who serves and worships an idol, as his or her god. It could be a cow, a wooden or graven image, a Shrine, a Monk, a house(s), a car or money.

Worshipper B—this is a person who goes to church, talks a lot about God, but does not have a personal relationship with His son Jesus Christ. However, he or she engages in religious programs, outreach ministries and related community services. He or she does good works, but has a worship capacity that is rather superficial.

Worshipper C—this is a person who says he or she is called by God, is born again, and is a follower of Jesus. He or she claims to walk in observance of God's word. This individual is properly clad and looks the part of a worshipper, but portrays a behavior like that of the world. He or she plays a good role – going to church frequently, while leading and functioning in certain ministerial positions, but finds it easy to be a partaker of worldly fancies instead of being led by the Holy Spirit. This type of worshipper serves and worships God from afar off, with little or no conviction.

And though there would be an urge and a desire to be sincere, the impact of worldly attractions heavily influences this type of worshipper. He or she lacks the discipline and commitment to live a holy and righteous life. If such a worshipper keeps on fooling himself or herself, sad will be their end. What makes it sad is that some individuals often say that Anguilla is a "Christian nation". Definitely, that is not so, at all. Christ advocates righteous living. If any nation promotes unrighteous life styles, then where does that put us? Are we still a "Christian nation?

Such a worshipper praises and worships God mainly when fast rhythmic songs are sung, and when the music is hot enough to make one dance, jump and shout. He or she gets all worked up, gets tired and, after a short while, has had enough. He or she then sits down and easily become distracted. Short-winded in spirit, there is no endurance. This pattern continues into the next service without change.

Micah Stampley's song, Holiness, carries a message that bodes well for such a worshipper:

Holiness, Holiness

Verse 1

Holiness, holiness is what I long for,
Holiness is what I need.
Holiness, holiness is what you want for me.

Verse 2

Righteousness, righteousness is what I long for

Righteousness, righteousness is what I need

Righteousness, righteousness, is what you want for me

Chorus

So, take my heart and mold it.

Take my mind, transform it,

Take my will, confirm it,

To your, to yours, oh Lord.

Verse 3

Brokenness, brokenness is what I long for

Brokenness, brokenness is what I need

Brokenness, brokenness is what you want for me

Worshipper D—this individual is a true and genuine worshipper who goes beyond the dance and shout. His or her worship transcends the jumping. This type of worshipper senses the need to, as it were, to make love to God, expressing with all that is with him or her, appreciation and love to a gracious, almighty God. This worshipper is characterized by singing intimate songs of love directly to the Father.

As this worshipper continues in real and true worship, he or she begins to sense the thickening, heavy presence of the Spirit of God coming down and filling the atmosphere. God's presence fills the room. This happens when one worships God in Spirit and in truth, according to John 4:22-24. The presence of God in a Spirit-filled atmosphere brings transformation, revelation, healings and miracles along with other spiritual benefits. This type of worshipper intimately worships the Lord in Spirit and in truth. We can't settle for anything less.

Some Principles that will help to keep us prepared for worship:

a. Develop a spiritual mindset—as opposed to having a mindset on fleshly or material things.

b. Make it a point of duty to pray for God's intervention in the service each time. Perhaps you could do so while driving to your house of worship.

c. Concentrate on the Lord – not on someone or anything else that can distract you.

d. Maintain an awareness of God's presence. His nearness is there waiting for you to recognize Him.

e. Purify your mind and be in humbleness of spirit. Meditate on God's goodness. Pray for a spirit of oneness and unity amongst the congregation before the start of service and for Him to reveal Himself.

f. Lastly, we must seek the guidance of the Holy Spirit and allow Him to lead. As you follow His unction, you will find that He will give you the right direction and revelation for the order of service.

Worship has always been a matter of divine ordinance under Patriarchal Law. For example, the worship that Cain and Abel rendered, according to Genesis 4. But God has specific requirements for worship under the Law of Christ. In this dispensation, we are to worship according to truth – not according to our own desires but with a devoted heart and with the right objective. We must accomplish the act of worship in the Spirit – not self. Worship must be conducted according to truth with reality. When relating our worship to scriptural principles, we must strive for accuracy and correctness as defined by Almighty God in the Holy Scriptures.

Remember the woman from Samaria at Jacob's well? At some point in their conversation, Jesus said unto her: "Woman, believe me, the hour cometh when ye shall neither worship on this mountain, nor yet at Jerusalem, worship the Father. You worship what you do not know; we know what we worship for salvation is of the Jews. But rather, the hour is coming and now is when the true worshippers will worship the Father in Spirit and in truth, for the Father seeks such to worship Him".

The Samaritans were ignorant about worshipping Jehovah rightly. Jesus told the woman: "Ye worship, ye know not what. We know what we worship, for salvation is of [us] the Jews." Jesus was explicit in His declaration about what true worship in the Spirit really is. The woman's claim that she worshipped after Abraham's custom was of no relevance to Christ. Christ had come to bring a new order and to revolutionize the hearts and mind of those who were ignorant. As the author of truth, He was forthright in teaching her a lesson about the true theology of worship – that is directed towards God the Father, through the Holy Spirit. If there are true worshippers, then logically, there are also false worshippers, and it behooves us to be the former.

Chapter 16:

"End-Time True Worshippers"

God is Seeking True Worshippers in These End Times

I hear The Spirit of the Lord saying: This is the time and season when God is ushering His worshippers and moving them into ranks for specific purposes. God wants end-time worshippers to be aware that worship must be directed towards Him in full adoration of Himself as the supreme, sovereign ruler of this universe. What follows are three important notes that have been revealed to me in accordance with pure, unadulterated worship.

Note 1:

Songs like: "Only You Are Holy; You are Alpha and Omega; Worthy is the Lamb"; and "There is None like you" can no longer be sung until we have stopped for a moment to really search our hearts and allow God to remove anything or any other god that is in our spirits, minds, and souls. We must begin to focus on the words of worship songs and recognize to whom we are singing them, if we are to really worship God in Spirit and in Truth.

It is time we bring our Spirit-man in alignment with holy and righteous living before Almighty God. It is a time to decree; a time to declare; and it is a time to advance in new dimensions in the Lord.

When our Spirits are connected to God, then strongholds and chains will be broken instantly, healings will take place and deliverance will happen, when least expected. At that time, signs and wonders will beam forth; miracles and supernatural manifestations will be the vehicle of God's awesome outpouring of His Holy Spirit upon the earth.

When we begin to clear our inner being and truly give God true worship, then and only then, will these dimensions begin to open up. The environment will change and conditions in the atmosphere will be corrected. Our communities, schools and homes will be transformed and the Church will move into its rightful position for the return of Jesus.

Note 2:

I hear the Spirit saying: There's going to be a domino effect when we, the sought-out worshippers, will move from the Outer Court into the Holy Place and worshippers from the Holy Place will move to the Holy of Holies. It is in these dimensions that we will experience the great move of God, demonstrating His power supernaturally, and moving us from glory to glory unto perfection.

The Outer Court worshippers are worshippers who feel comfortable on the outside of the temple with animals and every outward influence. But God will make room for new converted worshippers upon whom He will pour out of His Spirit. God says, "In the last days, I will pour out my Spirit upon all flesh". And this continuous supernatural move of God will cause: 1. The new Outer Court worshippers to move into the Holy Place; 2. The Holy Place worshippers will move to the final position; and 3. The Holy of Holies worshippers, the ones who carry the anointing to manifest signs and wonders.

Of course, the temple veil has been torn down so that every man can go before God for themselves, and a priest is no longer necessary to go before God on our behalf.

The Glory of God will be witnessed in "real time", similar to the movement of a stream or river. This glory will be a continuous flowing of joy, peace and contentment in God. And although some natural streams and rivers dry up from the effects of climate change, this stream of God's glory will never run dry but will keep springing up into living resources. Even in the midst of chaos, true worship will prevail in the atmosphere of the Holy of Holies. I declare and decree that true worshippers everywhere, universally, will be impacted by this new wave of God's glory as worshipers assume their position in the "Holy of Holies".

It is not that these signs and wonders are not happening now, but they will later become the norm with greater acceleration. Let us be sensitive to the Spirit now, more than ever, and begin to pay attention to what God is doing in the earth during these perilous times.

Note 3:

Concerning worship in the Holy of Holies, I hear the Spirit of the Lord saying: "There's going to be a supernatural "shuffling" that will affect the lives of God's people, like never before. We are all aware of the modern-day spiritual terminology known as "shift". Well, the Spirit says that the cycle of the "shifting" process will be replaced by the process of shuffling in order to bring the church to a state of readiness for Christ's return.

For the past years, the church and the world at large have undergone "shifts" of various types. We've had the paradigm shift, demographical shift, economical shift, global shift, Clarion shift— this shift and that shift.

"Shift" is the moving from one area to another or the separation and displacements of elements in a whole unit an organism. But "shuffle", in the spiritual sense of the word, is a process of a continuous righteous marching movement, together, advancing to a final designated position of stability, unity and perfection in God.

I must prophetically declare that through the spiritual "shuffle" there is going to be a continuous united movement towards specific goals, and there will be a process of positioning and adjustment, until the Kingdom Agenda is realized. All of God's people will begin to hear, see and speak the same thing in agreement — in unison. Walls of division will tumble down, and we, as believing worshipers, will be infused in the Spirit of oneness and unity. This will be the last day "pouring out" of God's

Spirit on all flesh. God will use the process of spiritual shuffling to accomplish this.

Gone are the days when we come into the House of God, and into His presence, with dirty minds, dirty mouths, dirty feet and hands and with deceptive hearts. God is causing His worshippers to advance before Him as one. When true worshippers worship God in unison the "shuffle" begins and God is glorified. And as we major in adorning Him with our worship, our God will bask in His glory, which He has created for His good pleasure.

Radiation Glory

Worshippers are being born and spiritually wired to carry the anointing and the glory of God, as one, and to bring changes in every aspect of our lives. The Spirit states that the kind of glory which will result from this unified trend of worship is called "Radiation Glory". It means that God will cause the worshipers' physical bodies to become adaptable to supernatural power so that, as durable instruments of a God, they would be able to ward off certain climate change diseases. God says that such diseases will not affect His worshippers' physical beings. All will be well with true worshippers physically, mentally, emotionally, economically, and otherwise.

This experience of "Radiation Glory" will cause true worship to vaporize before the heart of God as a pleasant, sweet-smelling savor to His sovereign nostrils. The glory of God will be made transferrable throughout the four corners of the earth. It will be such a time that whenever and wherever that glory is experienced in one part of the world, it will eventually affect other areas simultaneously. This presence represents a radiation or reflection of God's glory. It is the manifest touch that comes when the glory of God is radiated or transferred from a particular place to another. This is how God will be glorified in all the earth.

Everything will work for the good of God's people. However, by the same token, evil will escalate for a time. In the end, though, God in His great mercy has promised His people that He will trump evil with the power of good, causing hope and His peace to stabilize us and to be the anchor of our souls.

Running the Race to the End

I believe that in these times and in this season, there is a need to simply encourage all worshippers to endue to the end. There is a well-known bible verse, Matthew 24:13, which says, "the race is not for the swift." Rather, it is for those who endure to the end. Just as this saying relates to our everyday lives, it also applies to our spiritual journey in Jesus Christ.

Worshippers, in particular, must know that if you have started the race to follow Jesus Christ, it is not good enough to begin the run and then fall out by the wayside. Many believers have good beginnings, but few have good endings of spiritual fulfillment. In light of this, I would like to personally encourage *backsliders* to come back to their first Love before mercy door closes. You may have given up due to circumstances, but God is willing, ready and able to restore you.

Maybe you have lost trust in someone along the way. Or, you have been disappointed in someone or through something. Perhaps, it was the loss of a job, loss of a loved one, or maybe, you have experienced some form of sickness in your life. You are simply *discouraged*. Whatever you are going through, with your faith in Christ you can regain your steps and recover it all in Jesus' name.

At this juncture, I wish to launch an extensive "Word of Encouragement" to persons who have been in the faith for a very long time, but who have been affected by discouragement. It is obvious that some people give up on Christian service due to some kind of offence that has arisen in the church. Many a church member who had been called to the ranks of a worshipper has given up due to indifferences with another brother or sister. They have given up on worship, given up on service, and have become cold or lukewarm in the House of God.

In these times, when Christians seem to be so relaxed, comfortable and complacent, I am gently, yet sternly appealing to you to ARISE!

Human propensity is to become tired, bored, offended and weary at times. We are enthused by crusades and revivals, especially those conducted by overseas ministers, but then we relapse into a state of complacency and a "lukewarm" mode not long after the crusade has past. Our faith becomes boosted by revivals but when they have past we lapse into a state of spiritual doldrums.

Being spiritually exhausted is nothing new. Even the prophet Isaiah of old sounded the "wake-up call" to the complacent Israelites, in Isaiah 60:1, when he said, "Arise and shine for you light has come, and the glory of the Lord is risen upon you." If we are to see the glory of God exhibited among us in this 21st century, then we too must be actively working along with God to bring his glory unto the earth.

Yes, the best of us becomes spiritually exhausted at times. We may regard our spiritual burnout as an attack of the enemy, or perhaps merely a melancholy mood. In fact, we would have heard about the prophet Elijah, a powerful messenger of God, who was chased by the wicked queen Jezebel. As strong and as powerful as Elijah was in his walking with God, his faith fainted and he became fearful and discouraged over the wicked queen's pursuit after him. She had threatened to kill him. God had to send an angel to minister to this mighty, despondent prophet in his state of depression – to stir him up, revive him and give him the victory, according to the story in 1 Kings 19.

Every child of God must be active, and doing his or her part to bring God's kingdom agenda to fruition upon the earth. This is no time to give up or to be complacent about serving the Lord. Just as we devote ourselves to our regular careers and our secular jobs, we need to find time to bring glory to God by actively doing something for Him in order to advance of His kingdom. As Christians, it is our duty to serve Christ; as Christians, living to promote the cause of Christ is not an option, but a command. So Brother, Sister, I gently implore you to Arise. Rise and be restored in the name of Jesus. Don't give up the race now, but continue in the run.

Do you want to see souls saved? Do you want people to catch a glimpse of Christ like you had? Do you want to see your family and friends partaking of the free salvation that you are partaking of? Then come! Arise, get active and lift up Jesus. He made us a profound promise in John 12:32, where he said: "If I am lifted up from the earth, I will draw all men unto me." So, if you have been a worshipper, it is time to renew your commitment and continue to lift Him up.

I realize that after some period of time, one is susceptible to become burnt out. You ultimately drop out of the race, for one reason or another. You were, at one point, excited and full of joy. But now you are slowly losing that joy. Your excitement and zeal for God is being diminished.

I refer to this condition as being in **"the four D's state"**: *Discouraged, Despondent, Dull and Despressed*. But while in this state, you must do all you can to renew your faith and relationship with your Heavenly Father. He has not stopped loving you, and assuredly, He will never leave you. I pray and trust that as you determine to renew your position in the race, God will restore, refresh and replenish you.

No matter what experience you have had when you initiated your walk with Christ, you can regain that same fervor once again. Your faith can give you victory. So, whether you are a singer, sing for the cause of Christ. Occupy your time in song to God's honor and glory. Let the beauty of your voice be a sweet smelling savor for the pleasure of your King. Let others hear you sing about Him, so that they would be moved to worship Him too.

If you are a musician, pick up your instrument again and play it for His glory. Let the world hear the joyful sound of music unto your sovereign Lord. Use your talent for Him. If you are a worshipper, determine to worship Him in Spirit and in truth. That is the way He wants you to honor Him.

If you are just a regular member of His church; if you are just an ordinary part of his body, the Body of Christ, think not for one moment that your service to Him is only trivial and not vital. You can – and should – find opportunities to speak about His marvelous grace and his love to whomever you come into contact with, as the Holy Spirit leads you. Do not be afraid or ashamed to speak to people about the love which caused Jesus to lay down His life to purchase your salvation, and redemption for all mankind.

In the end, I encourage you, even as the Apostle Paul admonished the Romans to utilize whatever gifs and talent God had had bestowed upon them for His cause. Paul told them: "Having gifts differing according to the grace that is given to us, let us use them: If for prophecy, let us prophecy in proportion to our faith. Or ministry, let us use it in our ministering; he who teaches, in teaching; he who exhorts, in exhortation; he who gives, give with liberty; he who leads, lead with diligence and he who show mercy, do it with cheerfulness," according to Romans, 12:6-8. So, exercise yourself in using the gifts and talents God has given you for His hour and glory.

Exercising Gifts and Talents in the Race

It is very clear that a person who has been given gifts and blessed with talents to operate under the influence of the Spirit will be certainly endued with supernatural powers. Such a person will be mindful to equip himself with biblical directives in order to work for the benefit of the church, and the Kingdom on a whole.

The powerful functioning of gifts and talents under the direction of the Holy Spirit will be the new order in these last days. Men and women of God will utilize their gifts and talents to propagate the gospel of Christ throughout the world, and to worship Him with purpose and passion.

We are living in a realm which will propel us into spiritual acceleration. It is a movement that will transform the body of Christ from glory to glory, unto perfection, and ultimately prepare us for His return. As the scripture says, "This message of the Kingdom must be preached to the entire world, to all nations, for a witness and then shall the end come." (Matthew 24:14) This mandate will usher in the Rapture of the Church.

I end this session of motivation by quoting the words of this immortal hymn written by Daniel March in as far back as 1868. It is a rather long, song but its words carry an ever-living message:

Hark the Voice of Jesus

Hark the voice of Jesus calling,
Who will go and work today.
Fields are ripe and harvests waiting,
Who will bear the sheaves away
Long and loud the master calls us,
Rich reward he offers free.
Who will answer gladly saying,
Here am I send me, send me.

If you cannot cross the ocean,
And the distant lands explore.
You can find the lost around you,
You can help find them at your door.

If you cannot give your thousands,
You can give the widow's mite.
What you truly give for Jesus,
Will be precious in his sight.

If you cannot speak like angels,
If you cannot preach like Paul.

You can tell the love of Jesus,
You can say he died for all.

If you cannot rouse the wicked,
With judgment dread alarms.
You can lead the little children,
To the saviors waiting arms.

If you cannot be the Watchman,
Standing high on Zion's wall.
Pointing out the path to heaven,
Offering life and peace to all.

With your prayers and with your bounties,
You can do what heaven demands.
You can be like faithful Aaron,
Holding up the prophet's hand.

If among the older people,
You may not be apt to teach.
"Feed my lambs" said Christ our shepherd,
Place the food within their reach.

And it may be that the children,
You have led with trembling hands.
Will be found among your jewels,
When you reach the better land.

Let none hear you idly saying,
There is nothing I can do.
While the loss of earth is dying,

And the Master calls for you.

Take the task he gives you gladly,
Let his work your pleasure be,
Answer quickly when he calls you,
Here am I send me, send me.

Three Questions You Must Ask in Running the Race

Question 1 – What was it that drew you to your "first love", Jesus? Was it that you heard of heaven and its splendor and wanted to go there? Was it a mother's prayers, or a mentor whom you looked up to? Was it an answered prayer, or a miracle of God? What was it that drew you to Jesus, in first place? Perhaps you were like me – you heard a sermon on hell and all of the bad things that are associated with the place where worms do not die and where the fire is not quenched. Well, I decided that I didn't want to go there, so I accepted Jesus as the sacrificial Lamb of God who laid down His life to purchase my redemption.

If you have strayed in your relationship with God, there is still hope for you because He has His arms wide open, ready to receive you. Please, do not remain in a divorced state, estranged to God

Almighty. He is willing to remarry you all over again. (Hosea 14:4 and Jeremiah 3:22).

Worshippers: Now, when I talk about worshippers, I am not referring to an artist who entertains people, or a person who sings, or even leads worship in church *per se.* While these may be part of worship scheme, I am referring to believers who have accepted Jesus as their personal Lord and Savior. When you have done that, it is your duty to give God worship that belongs to Him. This is done through prayers, spiritual songs, reading of His word and being a witness by your lifestyle. By giving of your time, gifts, talents and your financial resources you would be fulfilling the will of God in your service to Him. Worshippers use their faith to serve God by paying obeisance and homage to sovereign ruler of this great universe.

Question 2: Where do you want to be at the end of time? I am sure many of you have thought about your eternal destiny and have asked at one time or another: where would I be at the end of my life or at the end of time. What have you done to ensure your foundation stands secure, and that you are conscientiously prepared to meet your Maker, dead or alive?

It is important to remember that living one's life in the fear of God is a lifelong race. It is not like a physical, temporary race or like running a marathon, per se. It is a race that calls for life-long endurance. One must have the willingness to be consistent in the run. In running this spiritual race, one must make sure he or she runs consistently, patiently, audaciously, courageously and with spiritual bravery. As believers, let us consider the race that is set before us, to run it with patience, always looking unto Jesus who is the author and finisher of our faith. (Hebrews 12:1-2)

Obviously, as we run for here and now, we are buffeted by the winds of opposition that blows vehemently against our faith. We may become disheartening at times, but it will be worth it all when we see our Redeemer, Jesus Christ. Be encouraged by this old hymn of the Christian faith:

Now that you have established where you're at in the race, the third question is this:

Question 3: How are you going to make your life count in terms of receiving your eternal reward? The scripture admonishes Christians to lay up for themselves treasures in heaven, instead of hording up wealth down here on earth. (Matthew 6: 19-21).

Here is where ranks and positions come into play. Whether you are rich or poor, bear in mind that it is not enough to make it to the finishing line empty handed. But your work here on earth should be well deserving of your reward in Heaven. There, according to your earthly works, you will be rewarded many folds, whether it be a ten-fold, twenty-fold – up to a hundred-fold. Your reward will be given to you by the Master, according to your work, as part of the Kingdom agenda here on earth.

Again, the scripture tells us what to expect at the finish line. It is essential to realize that God will reward you at the end of the race, depending on your quality of work while you have been active in service to Him. Ideally, this end-of-race reward is not like a promotion in a secular job here on earth. Instead, it is our work as servants, stewards and as worshippers while on earth that will determine the quality of reward that God will distribute to us in Heaven at the end of the race. (Matthew 16-27)

One big difference between the secular race and the spiritual race of the Christian life is that while the secular race consists of a standard distance, for fair competition, say 200 yards, 400 yards, one mile or a fixed-distance marathon which all runners have a chance to fairly compete in, the race that is of a spiritual nature, on the other hand, is one of various distances.

In some cases, for example, one may serve the Lord faithfully for five years and the Lord calls him or her home. Their race ends there. But others may be running for twenty, thirty or forty years, before they reach the finish line. However, God will not reward the runner according to the quantity of years served, but rather according to the quality of service given over that period of time that they have served.

The scripture speaks of a landowner who one day sent out laborers to work in his vineyard. Some of these workers labored for longer periods than others who agreed to work for just a few hours. In the end, the landowner paid all workers according to his discretion, based not upon the length of their service but according to the quality of their work.

And so, whether the Lord calls a runner home by the way of death, or whether the race ends when the lord returns, he will give to each of His workers (runners) their rewards according to the quality of their work. As the scripture says, "For the Son of Man shall come in the glory of His father, with His angels; and then He shall reward every man according to his works." (Matthew 16:27) That is the Word of God, and His Word is infallible. Mark you, it says "according to his works – not depending on who long he had served.

So, in order the gain an appreciable reward from the Lord, one must serve faithfully. One cannot be loose and unfaithful in service and expect to receive a brilliant reward from the Master. Hear what God's Word declares again:

He is speaking in the parable to the steward who had been faithful in his work: "And so, he that had received five talents came and brought another five talents saying: 'Lord, you delivered to me five talents. Behold, I have gained five talents more besides them. His Lord said unto him, well done my good and faithful servant. You have been faithful over a few things. I will make you a ruler over many things. Enter into the joy of your Lord." Matthew 25:21-23).

Saints of God, it pays to be faithful in your service to the Lord. Whatever you do in his vineyard, do it with all you might and continue doing it. Continue! Continue! Do not grow weary in well doing, for as the scripture says, "You shall reap if you do not faint." So no matter how many years the Lord has given you to serve Him in, no matter how long your race might be, run. Just run. Run faithfully and serve Him continuously. "Run with patience the race that is set before you, looking unto Jesus, the author and finisher of your faith.

Let us not flinch in our faith while we run. The race may be quite exhaustive at times, but let us keep our eyes on the prize, with the persuasion that, at the end, it will be worth it all.

Esther Kerr Rusthoi was a great stalwart of Christian service who faced many hardships during her race. In 1941, she penned the words to this enlightening hymn:

It Will Be Worth it All
Sometimes the day seems long,
Our trials hard to bear.
We're tempted to complain,
To murmur and despair.
But Christ will soon appear,
To catch His bride away.
All tears forever over,
In God's eternal day.

Chorus
It will be worth it all when we see Jesus.
Life's trials will seem so small when we see Christ.
One glimpse of His dear face, our trials will erase,
So bravely run the race 'til we see Christ.

At times the sky seems dark,
Without a ray of light.

We're tossed and driven on,
No human help in sight.
But there is one in Heaven,
Who knows our deepest care
Let Jesus solve your problems,
Just go to Him in Prayer.

Life's day will soon be o'er
Our storms forever past.
We'll cross the great divide,
To glory safe at last.
We'll share the joys of Heaven,
A harp, a home a crown.
The tempter will be banished,
Well lay our burdens down.

While running the race, the best of us may run with
our flames growing dim, and indeed, we grow
weary. I invite you to listen via YouTube to this
encouraging song, "Runner", by Twila Paris. It is
hoped that it will boost the endurance of those
who are weary in the race:

Runner

Courier valiant, bearing the flame
Messenger noble, sent in his name
Faster and harder, run through the night
Desperate relay, carry the light, carry the light

Runner when the road is long
Feel like giving in, but you're hanging on
You will run into His arms
Feel like giving in, but you're hanging on
Oh runner, when the race is won
You will run into is arms

Obstacle ancient, chilling the way
Enemy wakened, stoking the fray
Still be determined, fearless and true
Lift high the standard, carry it through, carry it
through

Mindful of many waiting to run
Destined to finished, what you've begun
Millions before you cheering you on
Godspeed dear runner, carry it home, carry it home

It is good to know that during your race, God has a
responsibility too – faithful to keep that which we
have committed to Him against that day. It is all a
part of His Kingdom agenda. The word of God says,
He who has started a good work in us, is able to
complete it to the end – to the finish line. So, as
God causes the "shuffling" process to continue, and
as we march forward like an army, soaring like
eagles, and advancing into new dimensions while
we run, let us decree and declare the Sovereignty
of God, and the hope that He has given us to make
it to the finish line. Remember that He is your

present help, and when you require help in the race you can look to Him.

Please read and listen to this song, "Help me", by Russ Taff. May you be blessed by it.

Song: Help Me

Lord, help me walk another mile
just one more mile
I'm tired of walking by myself
And lord, help me smile another smile
Just one more smile
I know I can't make it on my own

Chorus
Never thought I needed help before
I thought that I could get by – by myself
Now I know I just can't take it anymore
So with a humble heart, on bended knees
I'm begging you, please help me

Come down from your holy throne to me
Lord to lowly me
I need to feel the touch of your tender hand
Remove the chains of darkness
And let me see, Lord let me see
Just where I fit into your master plan – **(Jeremiah 29:11)**

Never thought I needed help before
I thought that I could get by – by myself
Now I know I just can't take it anymore
So with a humble heart, on bended knees
I'm begging you, please help me

To all worshippers, prayer worriers and intercessors: Now is the time to arm ourselves with the anointing. Most of the time, we only talk of the presence of God, but what about the anointing of God? It is the Spirit's anointing that breaks yokes and bondages from us and the people that are around us – those people whom we may be asked to pray for.

In such cases, we need to pray with the anointing. One must be anointed to change and shift an atmosphere in prayer meetings and worship services. We sing certain songs with good titles but the anointing is not there to affect the change pertaining to what we are singing about. Sure, the singing may good enough for a shout, a dance and a good feeling, but not anointed enough to the extent that it would create or bring change beyond our emotions.

We recall Jesus, Himself, who claimed in Luke 4:18: *"The Spirit of the Lord God is upon me, and he has anointed me to preach good tidings unto the meek; he hath sent me to bind up the*

brokenhearted, to proclaim, liberty to the captives, and the opening of the prison to them that are bound." Yes, in order to do God's work on earth, one must be empowered with **the anointing.**

The presence of God is everywhere. And while many people liken His presence to "goose bumps", He is spiritually tangible and it is much more than just goose bumps. Wherever God's presence is there is liberty to perform and to do His work. His work can only be done through us, as his vessels, who are **anointed** and set aside for his purpose.

At times, all it takes is one revelation from God to see a new manifestation of His abundant glory. Don't ever forget that a new revelation will bring new manifestation of God. We need to continually seek Him for fresher and clearer revelation for a greater and more powerful manifestation of His Glory in these last days.

I believe that as you read this book, God is revealing some things and promises to you. There may be some things that you have sought God for over the years, and it may seem that He has forgotten about them. No, He hasn't! He is just waiting for you to realize that your dream, your prophecy, your desire or your miracle is not dead.

God is ready to awaken those promises as you open up yourself to the glory of what He can bring to pass. I pray that as you are reading, the presence of God will come upon you to bring you into a deeper relationship with Him, and that you would be overcome with a desire to have a renewed mind towards God.

I have purposed in my heart, some years ago, that I will get so close to God that His very presence will be all over me, and that His Holy Spirit would always infiltrate my consciousness and my being. Whenever I go to any House of God, I want to be so saturated with his Holy Ghost's anointing that the devil will know that this child of God is filled with God's power. I am a carrier of God's presence, especially in sessions of worship and song. It is always my intention to let my song raise my praise and worship unto my Lord.

Worship brings us into God's abode. When the anointing seasons our worship, it brings change in people's lives. Anyone who comes into a place where the presence and power of God is moving will never leave the same way he or she came. It is my hope that my story and testimony would influence your life and change your lifestyle to be a sincere carrier of God's presence and anointing.

I hope that you will desire to follow the will of God for your destiny. As long as you place your life in his hands, he will bring your desires to past. God is waiting for you to take hold of the principles of His promises. Remember Proverbs 3:5-6 instructs you to: *"Trust in the Lord with all your heart and lean not to your own understanding. In all your ways acknowledge Him and He will direct your paths."*

I wish the same for you in the secular as I wish for you in the spiritual realm. Whatever your endeavors might be, since your life is in God's hands, He will work it out for your good so that you will meet your goals. One thing you should realize, though: when you have eventually reached you goal, by his help, do not ever neglect or forget to give Him the glory and praise. God is the giver of every good gift. His plan is to bless you and make you a blessing to others. Whatever you achieve is a blessing from Him. So remember to be humble as He continues to bless you.

Have you noticed that when some people are greeted and asked "how are you", their first response is usually, "I am blessed and highly favored"? However, people hardly speak of their ambition to broaden their relationship with the "Blesser". Why is it that so many people hold conversations about the goodness of God in reserve? The answer is that it takes one who is sensitive to the faithful acts of God to be able to tell of the experiences in relation to the One who has blessed them.

In these days of secularism, I am sorry to say that most people who wear the Christian label seem to be ashamed to mention "the Lord" in public. When they are in God's House, they would hide behind a song. They enjoy the music as the voices who join with them sing: "For all my life you have been faithful, for all my life you have been so, so good...with every breath that I am able, I will sing of the goodness of God." And they would mutter an 'amen' or two in a Sunday service, but on Monday morning they leave the Lord at home. They sing of Him in church, alright, but to mention Him and His goodness in the ear-shot of their friends or acquaintances is somehow socially unacceptable or politically incorrect. They seem afraid to offend those around them.

It is the anointing upon one's life that will enable him or her to declare God's goodness in wholesome conversation. Talking of God's goodness takes discipline with the utterance of words that come from a grateful heart. The discipline for declaring God's goodness comes through the anointing, and most Christians never attain to the experience of being anointed. So, they settle for the lesser value in responsiveness by saying, "I'm blessed and highly favored."

Due to a lack of the anointing upon the lives of average Christians today, the church, in general, is ineffective, and we are not seeing the manifestation of God's promises which He wants to endow upon us. Demonstrations of supernatural miracles are non-existent in the average church. God wants to breakthrough as he had done among the early Christians in the book of Acts, but Christians need to position themselves under the anointing of the Holy Spirit, even as the early church welcomed Him in the upper room, like a rushing mighty wind.

I believe that in these last days when secular spirits have overtaken many of our churches, we need to personally re-create upper room environments in our own lives. Whether this is done privately or corporately, there is a need for it in order to usher in the presence of the anointing in our churches. The anointing breaks the yoke – yokes of every kind, including the yoke of being ashamed and bashful to mention the Lord's name in public.

The spiritual goal here is to be anointed by the Holy Spirit. But in order to achieve this goal, Christians are to be thirsty enough to be filled. If we reflect on the believers in the Upper Room, Jesus had instructed them (his disciples) to stay together and "tarry". They were to wait, and waited they did, expectantly. These believers looked forward to the coming of the Holy Spirit. They were thirsty for Him, for they knew that, as the Comforter, He would represent the presence of Jesus Himself – Jesus who had dwelt among them as "God with us" for over thirty years. Do we want Jesus to be represented among us today? Think about it.

The Holy Spirit is the ambassador of Christ, so to speak. An ambassador is an agent who represents his native nation in a foreign land. Jesus was sensitive to the spiritual and social needs of His disciples. He knew that they would naturally miss His presence among them. So, being subject to His Father's authority, He told them that He was going away, but He said to them: "I will pray the Father that He will send you *another* comforter. And when He, the Spirit of Truth, is come he will guide you into all truth. " John 14:16.

One of the roles of the Holy Spirit is to guide believers into all truth, as Jesus prescribed, but another essential purpose of the Spirit, among so many others, is to anoint the believer. Just as God the Father anointed Jesus with the Holy Spirit, He, upon the request of His son, anoints us just as well, when we make ourselves available to be anointed.

Chapter 17:

"Recognizing the Power of the Anointing"

In Luke 4:18-19, the anointing is the burden-removing and yoke-breaking power of God. The anointing is what empowers a man or a woman of God to function supernaturally. The anointing enables Christians to do supernatural things according to God's mandate. We must understand that Christianity is a spiritual way of life, and the Christian requires God's anointing to function efficiently and effectively.

It is through the *anointing* that chains are broken and yokes are removed. Chains of oppression and depression; it is through the *anointing* that the yoke of sickness is destroyed and people are healed; captive souls are delivered and set free and broken hearts are mended.

The Spirit revealed to me that these twelve dimensions of the power of the anointing are applicable to Christians. These are essential for spiritual growth. While many of us may never be able to attain all of these powers, we must strive to excel in the Spirit and do our best to be equipped with them in order to be of greater service to the Lord.

The Twelve Levels of Anointing Power For Christian Growth:

1. The anointing power of praise and worship
2. The anointing power of a renewed mind
3. The anointing power of Pentecost
4. The anointing power of bodily sacrifice
5. The anointing power of the gift of Holy Spirit-with tongues
6. The anointing power of mountain-moving faith
7. The anointing power of God's wealth
8. The anointing power of the cross
9. The anointing power of God's love
10. The anointing power of forgiveness
11. The anointing power of repentance
12. The anointing power of prayer and fasting

The Power of Worship: Some of us will be gifted to sing unto the Lord, or play the kind of music that He is attracted to. And, as worship leaders, some of us would be used of God to motivate others, who are assembled before God, to worship along with us. The House of God is the ideal place or an appropriate location to worship, even though one may worship God anywhere or in private.

While God does not dwell in temples of brick or stone, He comes into His house through the person of His Spirit whenever a call to Worship is made. David was a Worship Leader, and he was always eager to go to the House of God. As he said in Psalm 122: 1, "I was glad when they said unto me, 'Come let us go into the House of the Lord.'" David wanted to utilize the power worship in order to commune with God and express his appreciation to Him.

The worship leader must be empowered to lead with the anointing. He or she must lead worship to move others' hearts to adore God in the Spirit. Worship must be done *in* the Spirit and *through* the Spirit. He who worships God must worship Him in spirit and in truth.

Why was David glad? It was because he knew that as he worshipped, the presence of the Lord would fill the House. He knew that worship would change a dreary atmosphere and bring about the tangible presence of God that would change the hearts of men through psalms and hymns and spiritual songs.

The Power of a Renewed Mind: As disciples of Christ, our minds must be renewed. Our minds must be determinately made up. Our minds must be so renewed that nothing and no one should influence us to backslide or to go against the will of God for our lives. A person with a renewed mind will certainly carry the power of the anointing as the Spirit dwells within. He or she will not waiver or doubt about their position in God. One with a renewed mind will stand the test of time, *not conforming to worldly things*.

The Power of Pentecost: Some of us will be so anointed by the Holy Spirit, and will be able to affect change in other people's lives, and the atmosphere, when we pray for individuals or speak to them in tongues, as the Spirit gives utterance – just as He did on the Day of Pentecost. The Pentecostal experience was witnessed by the apostles in the Upper Room when Jesus sent the Holy Spirit to fill, equip and empower believers to work for Him. "You shall receive power," Jesus said, "after the Holy Ghost is come upon you, and you shall be witnesses unto me..." according to Acts 1:8. The Power of Pentecost enables the anointed Christian to be a powerful witness for the Lord.

The Power of Bodily Sacrifice: The ability to be set apart for the peculiar purpose of being used of God enables one to have the power that comes about through bodily sacrifice. In Romans 12:1, Paul encourages us as follows: "I beseech you therefore, brethren, by the mercies of God that you present your bodies as a living sacrifice, holy and acceptable unto God which is your reasonable service." As a Christian, one must present his or her body as a living sacrifice, allowing the Holy Spirit to dwell in him or her richly. Christians in general must realize that their bodies are temples of the living God.

Once you have sacrificed your body and set it aside (consecrated it) to be used of God, you will be anointed and empowered against the urge to live a sinful lifestyle. Sins such as lying, stealing, fornication, adultery, alcoholism, gossip, etc., will have no place in a heart that has been anointed and empowered through bodily sacrifice. The Christian must seek to maintain spiritual holiness and righteousness – and to walk therein.

The Power of the Fruit of the Holy Spirit: The fruit of the Holy Spirit is the privilege given to Christians to bear the virtues of God, through His Spirit. It is termed as a fruit of nine segments, given to people who are anointed and have placed their faith in Jesus Christ. Such individuals are baptized and confirmed as members of the Body of Christ. When one possesses the fruit of the Spirit, the Spirit anoints him or her with the powerful qualities of: love, joy, peace, patience, kindness, goodness, gentleness, faithfulness and self-control, according to Galatians 5:22-23. God anoints that individual with a certain power – the Power of the Fruit of the Holy Spirit.

The Power of Mountain-Moving Faith: God has given to everyone a measure of faith, but when one trusts in the Lord and secures a deeper relationship with Him, God anoints him or her the Power of Mountain-moving Faith. This is the empowerment of the Holy Spirit that enables the individual to have victory through faith over life's circumstances as he or she trusts in God. Bear in mind that it does not take a whole lot of faith to move mountains or conditions of crisis proportions. Again, it does not depend on the *quantity* of your faith, but the *quality* of your faith, as you are anointed to exercise it. So, even "mustard seed faith" matters. Christ Jesus Himself promised in Matthew 17:20, "If you have faith as small as a mustard seed, you shall say to this mountain, 'Move from here to there and it will be removed."

God has anointed you with the power and authority to use His name to destroy the enemy, removing every mountain and trifling obstacle in our way. By using his name with a little child-like faith, you can conquer anything that was designed to harm you or bring you down.

The Power of God's Wealth: Through His Spirit, God anoints His children with the power to accumulate wealth either by using creative minds for business, by working with one's hands, receiving favor in a will made by relatives or associates, through leadership skills, or by tangible blessings as direct miracles – similar to Jabaz. Remember, Deuteronomy 8:18 says: "It is the Lord your God who gives you power to get *wealth."* Yes, God anoints the faithful believer with the power to work with his hands or his mind towards the goal of becoming rich. When we trust in the Lord, He will anoint us with the power and ability to attain wealth.

The Power of the Cross: The cross is a symbol of death the means life and the power of God's love to us. Christ's sacrificial death upon the cross is a direct provision to mankind, from the Father, through His son Jesus Christ. The scripture in John 3: 16 tells us: "For God so loved the world that He gave His only begotten son, that whomsoever believes on Him, should not perish but have everlasting life." The symbol of the cross is significant in demonstrating the sacrificial love of

Christ for us. Just as He laid down His life for us, we are called to be anointed by His spirit to take up our cross daily and follow His holy precepts. How amazing it is that we, as His followers, can receive the Power of the Cross that was provided for us over two thousand years ago at Calvary.

The Power of Love: Love is the ultimate attribute of God's nature. Because of God's love, when an individual chooses to accept Christ as Savior, he or she is born in the family of a loving God. The scripture calls this act of faith on the part of the individual being "born again" – being born of the water and of the Spirit, according to John 3:5. This new birth affords mankind the best gift of all – everlasting life.

Even as God, through Christ, has loved us, He expects us to have love for one another when we are anointed by His Spirit. Under this anointing, we take on His nature in our new family, the Family of God. Love is the powerful quality that indicates that we are disciples of Christ. Jesus Himself once said in John 13: 35 "By this will all men know that you are my disciples if you have love one for another.

The Power of Forgiveness: This is the power that enables us to be kind and compassionate to one another, even as God wants us to be. God's nature is one of love, and He requires that we forgive those who offend us, even as He forgives us. When Jesus was teaching His disciples to pray, a couple lines of that noble prayer says in Matthew 6:12: "...And forgive us our trespasses as we forgive those who trespass against us." When we have the anointing of the Spirit, it allows us to forgive our offenders. We must forebear with one another and release them, by God's grace, in the spirit of forgiveness. When we forgive, we are no longer under the power of the injury or the injustice that we would have experienced.

It was the Apostle Paul in his writing to the Ephesians who admonished: "Be ye kind one to another, tender hearted forgiving one another, even as God for Christ sake has forgiven you." Ephesians 4:32. Let us put this command in practice when we are offended by a callous brother or sister, and let us witness the freedom and release that the Power of Forgiveness can bring.

The Power of Repentance: The act of repentance involves two facets: 1. being sincerely sorry for the wrong one has done; and 2. turning away from repeating that wrong. Those who turn to God in prayer for the forgiveness of their sins must be remorseful before Him in an attitude of repentance. Repentance is wrapped up in one word: "humility". In order to be sorry, one must be humble. One cannot display a proud and hearty spirit while turning away and rejecting what's wrong. Rather, a spirit of sincere humility must be evident.

It is through the goodness and mercy of God that one is able to repent. Had it not been for God's goodness, His mercy and longsuffering, the act of repentance would be futile. When one repents before God for the wrong that he or she has committed, then God is willing to forgive.

The act of repentance is a serious thing. Every man is required of God to repent or perish. In Romans 2:4, we see the principle of repentance that is based upon God's love and goodness. The scripture here asks a sobering question, and implies a conscious reply.

Let us hear what Paul asks, and let us notice what he states: "Do you despise the riches of His goodness, forbearance, and longsuffering, not knowing that the goodness of God leads you to repentance? But because of your hardness and your impenitent heart, you are treasuring up for yourself wrath in the day of wrath and revelation of the righteous judgment of God." Let us be sensitive to Paul's admonition. Only the Power of Repentance can free us from the impending wrath of God in the day of judgment.

The Power of Prayer and Fasting: Prayer and fasting is powerful. The two go together to serve in restoring and strengthening one's intimacy with God, first and foremost. Purposes of prayer and fasting includes, but are not limited to: Developing spiritual strength; resisting temptation; developing self-mastery of our spirit man; bringing our bodies into subjection to the will of God, and empowering the Christian to do miracles as Jesus did.

Prayer and fasting enhances one's life. It promotes humility and demonstrates one's dependence on the Lord. Through prayer and fasting we obtain spiritual knowledge, guidance and purification of heart and soul. Fasting prepares and equips the Christian to do "exploit" for the Lord. The glory of God would be revealed from stage to stage when Christian practices a life of prayer and fasting.

The man or woman who spends time praying and fasting tends to hear from God better. Why? Simply because they have a more instantaneous connection with the Father. The power and presence of God increase upon you and your faith deepens if you are spending that time in prayer, in praise, worship, and in the word. During times of prayer and fasting, your spirit is totally focused on the spirit realm and distractions will lose their grip of you. Moreover, the Holy Spirit anoints one who prays and fasts with the power to overcome spiritual challenges. Jesus Himself once declared that certain great miracles cannot be accomplished unless one prays and fasts.

Jesus is our Master example. If He, the Son of God, found it necessary to fast and pray in the wilderness for forty days and forty nights, how much more do us as mortals need to emulate His example.

The scriptures give an account of a child who was possessed with a familiar spirit that tormented him day and night. His father approached the disciples with the optimistic hope that they would pray for his son and release him from the oppressive demon. The disciples prayed, alright, and they prayed intensely, but nothing happened. The child remained bound and possessed by the evil, demonic power. Note that I say it was a demonic "power". It would turn out that only the Power of Prayer and Fasting could deliver him from his perilous plight.

Well, the father of the boy, so disappointed by the disciples' effort, went directly to Jesus and explained the situation. Jesus got somewhat frustrated with the disciples and wondered if they expected Him to be always with them. After Jesus rebuked the evil spirit and freed the boy, the disciples came to him and asked, "Why could we not cast out that demon?"

Here is what Jesus answered in Matthew 17:21: "This kind [of demon] does not go out, except by prayer and fasting." We need to value the Power of Prayer and Fasting. Prayer is good. But there are instances where prayer alone can't cut it alone. If Jesus found it necessary to pray as well as to fast, all alone with His Father, we need to do so even more.

A personal testimony: The importance of being anointed

I take this opportunity to share a personal story of the importance of being anointed. **In 2010**, I had an encounter with a particular evangelist from Jamaica who had visited Anguilla several times before. On one of her visits, our church gave her the opportunity to conduct services at our ministry, The No-Walls Church of Hope. As a pastor, I was disappointed and offended when she adversely called me to the altar to pray over me.

She made a statement which did not depict who I am. Being troubled over the declaration which she made upon me, and knowing the warrior that I am in the Spirit realm, I consulted with the Holy Spirit about this "false prophecy". I asked Him to deal with this evangelist drastically, and to make her wrong, right publicly — to correct what she had pronounced on me.

Well, it turned out that a week later, my God vindicated me. The Bishop of this same evangelist visited Anguilla from Jamaica for a week of services at The Awakening Ministries Church in North Hill. During the worship session, the Spirit of the Lord was upon me, as I sang fervently in turbulent worship unto God. When the visiting man of God completed his message and was giving the altar call, this Bishop, whom I had never met before, and who definitely didn't know me, called several persons to come to the altar. It was as if the Spirit was giving him the discernment as to whom he should call forward.

Amazingly, he pointed in my direction and beckoned that I come. At first, I looked behind me, for certainly, he couldn't possible mean me. But he kept pointing in my direction. When I realized it was me, he was beckoning to, my mind went right to the episode that his associate evangelist had put me through a week earlier.

I was therefore somewhat hesitant when he summoned the usher to come over to the bench where I was sitting. He told me, "It's you he is calling." Oh boy! I said to myself on the spur of the moment, but the Holy Spirit assured me that I should not be afraid. So, with that, I went forward. At this time, he was praying for persons and ministering to their various needs. He was declaring over them the messages that the Spirit wanted to impart to them.

When it came my turn, I was the last individual standing there before him. As I am now typing what he said to me, I am again so overwhelm how God used this stranger to "right the wrong" that his evangelist had done to me.

The man of God touched my stomach and he declared seven solitary words in no uncertain terms: "Sister, there is nothing wrong with you." He then lifted my chin to look upwardly and profoundly said, "You have the Trumpet of God within you, and it is laced with the anointing." In addition, he stated: "When you sing, the atmosphere changes and some people will be offended because they are not on the level that you are at." He then gently told me to return to my seat.

Woooow! I walked back to my seat floating in the Spirit, as if I had just killed Goliath. What I saw next was the same evangelist who had made the evil pronouncement over me. She was on the floor laid out face down before God, as if in repentance.

Children of God, you must know who you are in Christ and whose you are. As long as you are living righteously, do not allow anyone to make any false pronouncements over you that are not of God and do not depict who you are in the Spirit. When they do, you have the obligation and the right to go before God and to plead your case against them and watch Him bring judgment or chastisement on whomever has denounced you. Watch God vindicate you. Hallelujah!

That is how many of my battles have been won throughout the course of my life. I praise God for that victory and even though that weapon was formed, it just couldn't prosper. Why? Because as a child of God, knowing my authority, contrary to that evangelist's pronouncement, it only gives significance to the scripture in Psalm 105:15 that says, "touch not my anointed and do my Prophet no harm."

I can rest assured that as long as you and I are in obedience to God and to His Holy Spirit, then His banner of protection and love will be over us. God's presence and power will defeat anyone and everything that the adversary uses to bring us harm or to bring us down. I am saying this with bold conviction in my God, and as Sinach song says: I know who I am.

I know who I am

I know who God says I am
What He says I am
Where He says I'm at
I know who I am

I'm walking in power
I walk in miracles
I live a life of favor
For I know who I am

We are a chosen generation
Called forth to show His excellence
All I require for life God has given me
And I know who I am

I am holy, I am righteous
I am so rich,
I am beautiful

I'm walking in power
I walk in miracles
I live a life of favor
For I know who I am

Seven lessons on how to protect the Anointing: Samson and Delilah

1**. Protect the anointing by knowing whom to run to when you are pressured**. Samson needed to stay consecrated and obedient to his spiritual calling and to his Nazarite vow. After been daily deceived, pressured and pestered by Delilah with her lustful words, he yielded to the temptation and told her that no razor ever came upon his head since he left his mother's womb. He gave away the very secret of his anointing and power. He admitted that if he was to be shaven, his strength would leave him and he would become weak and be like any other man. That was the end of his anointing.

2. **Protect the anointing by guarding your heart from outside forces**. Samson told Delilah all of the secrets of his heart. He did not resist the temptation that came upon him, but found it pleasurable to open his heart to her as an outside force again and again. He did not guard his heart. He was unlike Joseph, who did everything possible to escape from Potiphar's wife when she tried to lure him into her seducing trap.

3. Protect the anointing by staying humble – a life of humility. Samson woke up from sleep and said, I will go out as accustomed and shake myself as before. But the Spirit of the Lord had departed from him. Had he humbled himself and repented immediately, I believe God, by His grace, would have restored him to a wholesome state.

4. Protect the anointing by staying focused on goals while waiting on God. Samson was tied up and bound up by Delilah, and he was imprisoned. He was in a state of spiritual blindness, oblivious to his Nazarite upbringing and seduced by his commitment to Delilah.

5. Protect the anointing by remembering who you are in Christ, even when others taunt you. Samson was taken to a large arena to be taunted by the Philistines. They plucked out his eyes, and they mocked, laughed and jeered at him over his apparent defeat.

6. Protect the anointing by calling on God. Samson called to the Lord, saying, oh Lord God, remember me I pray. "Strengthen me I pray, just this once oh God, that I may with one blow take vengeance on the Philistines for the loss of my eyes."

7. **Protect the anointing by knowing where to put your hands**. Samson in the end took hold of two pillars which supported the temple. He braced himself against the columns and then said, "Let me die with the Philistines". What a terrible way to die. In the end, God in His mercy allowed Samson to use his strength one last time, but to his own peril.

We need the Spirit of discernment in these days to see, in the Spirit realm, and to know the works of the devil in our churches, in our schools, our homes and our communities. The ***anointing*** of the Spirit is really the game changer here. If Samson had that Spirit of discernment, he would not have fallen into that great plight.

Oh, how we need the ***anointing*** like never before! It is probably, the most important and effective vehicle that brings victory in almost every aspect of life for the people of God. If, for some reason, you were overtaken by temptation like Samson and you repented, God will forgive you. However, if you choose to continue giving in to the source that keeps causing you to fail like Samson did, sooner or later you too will bring shame and mockery upon yourself. Ultimately, you will forfeit what God intended for your life.

Whatever you perceive God to be, that is what He will be. If your focus is on Him as your strong tower, that is what He will be. If you deem Him to be your healer, then He would be your healer. God will meet you at the point of your needs. Whatever your image is of Him, He is faithful to confirm Himself to you for your good. It is the same with the anointing on your life. It is most important now, more than ever, to hold on to the anointing that God has blessed you with. That is the one aspect of your life that Satan is most interested in.

Let's look at Job. Satan asked God to remove the hedge from around him and he challenged God that Job will fail. Well, what did God do? He allowed the protection from around Job to be removed. Satan then went in for the kill, with his entire arsenal against Job. And we well know how the story ended. Job stood his ground even though he felt there were no answers to his prayers, and when it seems as though God was not near, he maintained his integrity in the Lord. He held on to his conviction, knowing who he was and whose he was. As a result, with great persuasion he penned these words in Job 13:15: "Though He slays me, yet will I trust Him."

Job made this statement when he was in a terrible season of pain and suffering in his life. He had lost all of his children, his wealth, and his health. Even his wife and friends mocked him. His wife went to the extent of telling him to curse God and die. His friends accused him of some sinful act he must have committed. But Job knew his God, as his sustainer, and he was convinced that his God would not put more on him that he could bear. He had hope in his God to see him through. You too can be assured that whatever you are going through, if you be as loyal as Job was, if you keep the faith and protect your anointing, then you can accomplish your mission in life, which He has given you.

The scripture ascertains that Satan is the prince of the power of the air, and he manages the spirit that work in the children of disobedience, according to Ephesians 2:2. There are so many vicious things happening around us which he is the author of. There is violence and crime and political unrest; there is gambling, prostitution, acts of fornication, broken homes and social unrest. Our societies are on the edge of moral decay. But, as the old Caribbean chorus says, "It's amazing what praises can do." So let us sing praises to our Father. His Holy Spirit will make a difference.

I am not telling you to do anything that I am not doing myself. I play pure worship music and do worship unto God on a daily basis. I gain many spiritual benefits by doing so. My spirit-man stays encouraged and refreshed, my mind stays at ease, my stress level is lower, and I allow God to work on my hopes and aspirations for my future.

And just in case you become tired of the repetitious radio songs, I would like to introduce you to a YouTube radio station named "K-Love", an American YouTube station. One humorous song on this station that inspires and motivates me is a song that says: "the devil wants to kick me out of the church but you can't take the church out of me." K-Love features songs to meet your every need.

Some of my favorite artists are: Richard Smallwood, Donnie McClurkin and the Gather Vocal Band, among so many others. Richard Smallwood sings a song that I would like to introduce. It's a song in which he says: "Thanks for waking me up this morning." I play this song repeatedly and religiously every day. Others like "Hold on Don't Let Go", "He's my Everything" and "Praises Wait for Thee" are among my favorites. These are just awesome songs that would fill your souls with praise and worship unto the Lord.

Remember, when we set ourselves to worship the Lord, He requires us to worship Him in Spirit and in truth. I notice that there are some church leaders and worshippers who indulge in certain lifestyles of fornication, adultery, lying, stealing and other unrighteous acts.

Righteousness needs to be our watchword and song. It exalts our nation, according to the scriptures. For the sake of promoting righteousness, I must be a mouth-piece to create awareness of the condition relative to our place in God. As an instrument of God's righteousness, it is my duty to encourage the wayward ones to turn from their wicked ways and turn to the Lord.

The Church Sets the Stage for Government's Success

Folks, we are the Church – the called out ones. We are the *ecclesia*. We must be separated from the world and consecrated to God who called us. As the *Body of Christ*, we are privileged in Christ. We were called to set the tone for Government through prayers, involvement in certain aspect of Government's ministerial social functions, especially to benefit the people in a holistic manner. In turn, the government would govern by and through the atmosphere set by the Church. Then, and only then, will God's favorable change will come to the nation.

Do you wonder why Government has to grapple in frustration with political and social unrest and divisive issues? Do you wonder why Governments are unable to work effectively for the good of the people they are supposed to represent and lead? Take a look at the condition of the Church. Now, I believe that if the people of Israel had listened to God when they asked Him for a king, things would have been in a more godly order under God and the prophets. But instead, the people wanted Saul to be their king, outside of God's desire.

That is not to say that any Government personnel, who wins the heart of the electorate, and is not God-conscious, will not govern for the good of the people. However, I believe that while many of these "politicians" take office with good intentions, based on the many promises they declare, they soon forget their promises. I have observed that because the hearts of many Government officers are deceitful, in first place, over time the manifestations of an insincere heart surfaces. It is then that we see them functioning contrary to their pre-election intentions. In 1 Samuel Chapters 13 and 16, we will see similarities of governing of this in the likes of Saul. And many other political leaders around the world have these characteristics.

Various spirits of political greed, ignorance, intimidation and democratic nuisances will be the order of the day in elections globally, and even in our very own Anguilla, if are not mindful of God's ordinances. And if the people do not rise up against the evil that is being perpetrated now, then the outcome will be upsetting divisions, confusion and uprisings of many forms. Political unrest will take place all around us, giving rise to social turmoil and moral decay.

The spirit of prophesy shows that overtime, these antisocial traits will become the norm for generations to come. How can we escape this? By simply being obedient to God's voice for the nation in this 21st century. As it was said before, righteousness must be our watchword. God honors us when we endeavor to practice righteous living. This should be the mandate for everyone – whether politician, parson, priest or peasant. God promises that His righteousness will lift us up or exalt us as a nation if we turn to Him. It is therefore time to repent before God and be determined that

His righteousness will uphold us and spare us from His wrath that is to come.

We can therefore see that God's Ministers and Leaders have a pivotal role to play when it comes to supporting and encouraging Government Leaders – so until we, the church, take our rightful place in society to pray for, interact with, and set examples before those men and women who are chosen and placed in authority to lead and govern, then they will not be inclined to follow after godliness and obedience to God's will. It is unfortunate though, that some church ministers are only interested in their own enrichment.

So, what are we going to do Church? May God help us to begin to know who we are, and whose we are in these times of threatening social unrest? As spiritual leaders, we have a key role to play in God's order for governments. As primary stewards of God in the earth, we are responsible to Him for the nation He has blessed us with.

We may have missed the mark over time, but God still expects His Church to repent and represent Him. We must begin to affect change in the realm of righteousness before Him. Remember what He says in His word: ***"Righteousness exalts a nation, but sin brings reproach upon a people."*** Proverbs 13:34.

Every believer in Christ, who lives by faith in Him, is "the righteousness of God in Christ". according to Corinthians 5:21. This means we are the expression of the characteristics of God. Righteousness brings us closer to Him, and it enhances fellowship with the Almighty God. God affords us power and authority in righteousness. Righteousness always brings us in God's presence. You see, since God has righteous characteristics, He is attracted to us when we manifest works of righteousness ourselves. Yes, He comes near, and His presence fills our very being when we endeavor, by the aid of His Spirit, to exercise the righteousness of His son in our daily living. Righteous gives us boldness to be victorious in battle.

Furthermore, righteousness not only exalts the nation, but it is also indicates the upright qualities of the people of God, within the nation, and points to their standing of holiness and purity of heart.

Self-righteousness, on the other hand, is a righteousness that comes from someone's own goodness and work. When one is self-righteous, he or she does not completely rely on the righteousness of Christ, but on his or her own doing. This kind of "righteousness" brings God no glory. To be truly righteous is to obey the commandments of God, as his son Christ did. As we mortals follows Christ's example, we become the righteousness of God in Him, we endeavor by His Spirit's help to live in a way that is honorable to Him. Psalms 106:3 says, how blessed are those who keep justice, and who practice righteousness at all times.

When we, the people of God, allow the Holy Spirit to govern our lives through truths and divine factors, then there will be change and growth; we will begin to preach the word of God rightly divided and in truth; we will teach Bible principles based on the truth; we will worship God in spirit and in truth; there will be healings and miracles done only in His name through intervention and truth; the church will begin to fear of God, and acknowledging who He is.

When we the people of God live righteous, holy and godly lives before mankind, and when we propagate and promote the gospel for the kingdom of God, only then will sinful reproaches be abated. Only then will the wrath and judgment of God be appeased, and nations will be exalted in righteousness.

Alas! Let us not lose hope and get weary in our endeavors. Instead, let us amend our ways in anticipation of a brighter future. May our politicians and people alike, be determined to arm ourselves as a nation of righteousness to fight against the forces of our evil foes. Let justice and righteousness prevail. And may the church be destined to continuously bear the hallmarks of righteousness before the world, to the pleasure and glory of God.

Chapter 18:

"Developing Your Mustard Seed Faith"

Mustard seed faith enables us to accomplish miracles – to move mountains. But if this small amount of faith is developed, how much more will the miracles that we would see? The basic principles of our faith must be in accordance with the word of God. The principles of faith are relevant for the success of our service and commitment to the Lord. As Christians, we look not to the things that are seen but to the things that are not seen. In 2 Corinthians 5:7 the Apostle Paul tells us: "For we walk by faith, not by sight".

According to God's sovereign commands in the Bible, the prominent roles of faith for Christian living are these: Faith is essential for salvation; hearts are purified by faith; we are sanctified by faith; and we are justified by faith. However, in order for our faith to truly work, we are to be in obedience to God, or else, we will be operating on *dead faith* and that kind of faith is not of God.

You see, everyone has faith in something and someone. Every person lives his or her life based on some sort of belief system. But our faith needs an object, something or someone in which to believe, trust, and have confidence in. And since it is only God who gave to every man a measure of faith, then it is only wise that we put our faith and trust in Him. He is the object of a Christian's faith.

What does faith look like in our lives today? How do we exercise faith, even our mustard seed faith in our daily lives? Are we able to trust God with our faith enough to see our mountains move? We better be exercising our faith and relying on God to be the source of everything we need. To do otherwise, we would be displeasing the Lord.

The scripture tells us in Hebrews 11:6 "Without faith it is impossible to please God, for he who comes to God must believe that He is, and that he is the re-warder of them who diligently seek Him. Faith comes by hearing the Word. When we hear the promises of God's Word or the gospel of Christ, hope arises within us and, like a child looking to the hand of his father, we become expectant in our faith and motivated to believe that what God has promised He will bring to pass. And, even though it might not come to pass overnight, with constant belief and the exercising of one's faith, needs will be met and aspirations will be accomplished.

Although the faith within us is a gift, it must be cultured and sought after until it grows from a tiny seed to a big tree. When God sees our effort in believing in Him, he helps us to expand our faith by the endowment received through the Holy Spirit. That is how our little faith – our mustard seed faith – is developed. That is how our faith grows.

The nature of faith is not a manmade thing, like material things and, furthermore, faith is not a visible or tangible element. Faith is the substance of things created through which we receive from God. Faith has to be developed.

Jesus is the Chief cornerstone of the Christians' faith, according to Ephesians 2: 20. Faith concerns the putting of your trust in God and having the confidence that He will fulfill His promises. Praying to God will build your faith and you will feel confident and strong. God Himself says that He will strengthen you and help you. Your prayers will never be bigger than your expectation in life. In other words, you just can't wish for a thing and it becomes what you wished for. Let your prayers be the vehicle by which you start your day, every day. When you do that, God said, He will uphold you with His righteous right hand, according to Isaiah 41:10.

As you grow, it is time to rejoice in the Lord always, pray without ceasing and give thanks in all things, for it is the will of God, in Christ Jesus for you, according to 1Thessalonians 5:16-18. Your faith will face some challenging moments that will sometimes cause you to doubt. There is no need to worry, for of course, this is all a part of your Christian growth as you mature in the ways of God. If there are no challenges and struggles in your walk of faith, it would be so much harder and virtually impossible to please God. As you begin to stir up your faith in God, acknowledging His presence in your life, then whatever you ask when you pray, just believe that you have it, and it will be yours, according to Mark 11:24. Stand fast in your faith! Be brave! Be strong and unmovable. And God says, fear not for I am with you, be not dismay.

Faith is the gift for justification, and faith enables more gifts to be added to our lives. When a person is born again, God gives him or her, the share or measure of faith as a new member of the family of God. We receive gifts from God according to the measure that God has given us, and we exercise the gifts to the same measure of our faith. Exercising our gifts in accordance to our faith cause us to experience great benefits, physically, socially, mentally and spiritually. Not everyone receives all the gifts, or the same measure of faith. God is sovereign and He distributes each gift according to the measure of that he bestowed on us. It is as He sees fit.

Many people struggle with a lack of faith, but God instructs us to have childlike faith in Him. As we develop that measure of faith, it will sometimes take us through difficult paths of trials and tests, but as the scripture says, according to Job 23:10, "But He knows the way that I take, and when He has tested me, I shall come forth as gold." Our faith, therefore, is not something we can produce in ourselves. It is a gift that comes directly from God, and sometime, like Job, we will have to go through the fires of life to be refined and prepared for greater service in God's kingdom. Amazingly, it is that fiery processing which causes our mustard seed faith to grow larger so that we are able to move even greater mountains.

It is important to note the faith will shape the way we live. When we put our faith to work, we will live loyally as we are committed to Christ. Our lives would be pleasing to God the father in all that we do. Remember, our faithfulness requires submission to Him, period. And it comes from a place of realizing that we are in need of a Savior. Submission can only happen if God has total control of our lives.

Chapter 19:

"Latter Days Out-Pouring for the Harvest"

It is written in Isaiah 2:2-3: "And it shall come to pass in the last days, that the mountain of the Lord's house shall be established in the top of the mountains, and shall be exalted above the hills and all nations shall flow unto it. And many people shall go and say, come ye, and let us go up to the mountain of the Lord, to the house of Jacob and he will teach us of His ways, and we will walk in his paths: For out of Zion shall go forth the law and the word of the Lord from Jerusalem."

When we think about the end times, we should not simply focus on the terrible things that are going to befall the earth. In the midst of these terrible things are wonderful happenings amongst God's people as well. There will be great manifestation of God's glory that will cause all nations to flow to God's house, causing many to turn to Him.

Habakkuk 2:14 says: "For the earth shall be filled with the knowledge of the glory of the Lord, as the waters cover the sea and Isaiah 60: 2-3 says, for behold, the darkness shall cover the earth, and gross darkness the people. But the Lord shall arise upon thee, and His glory shall be seen upon thee. And the Gentiles shall come to the light and kings to the brightness of thy rising. The glory of God that will cover the earth will not amount to a cloud that hovers over trees and mountains."

This will be the nature and power of God that will be manifested through our lives for the world to see. It is going to be an unprecedented move of God's power and glory through your life in these last days. I am not talking about a man, or any other gods out there. I am talking about the only wise, true, living, Almighty God, the creator and ruler of His universe.

As mentioned above, this latter rain out pouring will be unprecedented. The latter harvest rain is to bring maturity to that which God has planted in the earth. The purpose will be to empower the saints to preach the gospel of the Kingdom of God to every nation for a witness. The former rain referred to speaking in tongues during the first outpouring of Pentecost, when the Holy Ghost was poured out in the upper room and we see people from every part of the world were amazed and puzzled by every language spoken by the 120 people in wait to be endued by the power of the Holy Spirit.

The second outpouring of the Holy Spirit, referred to as the latter rain, will have a greater impact than that of the former rain. Joel 2: 23-27 talks about the latter rain to be poured upon the fields. It will destroy the locusts which had eaten the former crop. Joel is telling us that not only the fields will be restored, but, in the spiritual sense, God will pour out of His Spirit upon all flesh. Wonders and signs will be seen in the heavens and in the earth. And Zechariah 10:1 says, "Ask for the latter rain and He will make flashing clouds, sending showers of rain and providing grass in the fields for everyone." Yes, He will pour out, by His will, refreshing showers upon all those who are inclined to be saturated with the anointing of His Holy Spirit.

This outpouring of the Spirit and power will not come in mercy drops or drizzles, for the Lord will make flash clouds and pour out abundant showers of His blessings. The Holy Spirit's transforming power is going to refresh our beings. It will come about in good measure, pressed down, shaken together and running over. As He showers you with His uncommon favor, you will walk in the reality of His overflow to do exceedingly, abundantly above all that we can think or ask for, according to Ephesians 3:20.

The outpouring for the harvest is going to be plentiful, but when the harvest matures, the laborers needed to reap it will be few, as the scripture says. For this reason, Luke tells us in this era to earnestly pray to the Lord of the harvest to send out laborers into the vineyard for the reaping. We are laborers together with God, and according to 1 Corinthians 3:9, we are God's fellow-workers in His field, working together for the building up of His divine kingdom.

This reaping process will be similar to the parable of vineyard workers in Matthew 20:1-16, where the laborers who came to work in the field last were paid the same as those who had come to work from early morning at the beginning of the shift. The same glory of God will be seen here on earth for those who would be newly redeemed and converted as those older heads who had been converted years ago, and who have remained faithful to the call. New converts will earn equal rewards or pay, so to speak, along with those who were saved years ago. There won't be any reason to get jealous of the later converts.

That being said, it would be important to note that when Heavenly rewards are distributed, when we stand before God's throne, one's reward will be great according to his or her faithful service here on earth. And that does not just mean the length of time or years of service. No, not just the *quantity* of years served, but the *quality* of service for God in His Kingdom. Then will God say, according to Matthew 25:23, "Well done good and faithful servant, you have been faithful in a few things, and I will make you ruler over many things. Enter into the joy of your Lord."

Chapter 20:

"Rainbows – God's Covenant with Anguilla"

The rainbow is a phenomenal piece of God's creation. Mankind first witnessed the awe and beauty of the rainbow when God made a way for Noah and the inhabitants of the ark to step out on dry land after He had destroyed the wicked Antediluvian World by a dreadful flood, according to Genesis Chapter 9. God had established the rainbow with Noah as a promise that he would never destroy the earth again by a flood.

In 2014, I was inspired by the Holy Spirit to write a message pertaining to rainbows which are associated with God's mercy and his covenant for the island of Anguilla, where I have taken up residence for over forty years. Providentially, the Caribbean Island of Anguilla, the northernmost island in the Caribbean chain, is colloquially called *Rainbow City*.

The Lord had shown me the clear vision for the nation of Anguilla, but due to certain doubts, criticisms and rejection of the content of my written message, it was not published in the local news media as I had desired for it to be.

Well, here I am at this time, being motivated to create certain awareness. It is imperative that we pay attention to what God is saying to the nation of

Anguilla, in particular, as well as the surrounding islands in the Caribbean.

During the years 2014 thru 2016, we were frequently seeing a series of rainbows, which we could almost reach out and touch if it was possible. Some of them were single and others were some double, and they appeared at any time through the course of the day, sometimes several time a day. These phenomenal wonders of God's glory still appear, though not as frequently as they did over those three years.

I have been intent on searching them out with only a little bit of effort, because every time I would simply think of a rainbow, bam! Theirs is one! I began to pay keen attention to them, and anticipated observing them. It was like "chasing rainbows". For me, it became something to look forward to as I drove to and from work.

Some people would write off the occurrence of rainbows as trivial scientific dogma caused by the refraction of and reflection of light against droplets of water or moisture in the atmosphere. But anything can be scientific. There is also a scientific explanation for lightning and thunder, which result from emissions of electrical charges produced by weather patterns in the atmosphere. All that being said, it is safe to say that life itself is scientific. Our biological composition is a marvelous creation of God's magnificent glory. And the glory of rainbows is no different.

In admiring these splendid rainbows over Anguilla, something began stirring in my spirit. Then, I asked God what is the meaning of rainbows. Are they signs of some promise to Anguilla? They were indeed signs that manifested themselves all over this island, from east to west, and from north and south, as they were seen every day from sunup to sun-down.

In seeking the face of God concerning these rainbows, the Spirit revealed to me that God has a covenant with Anguilla, and like Israel, we too are a blessed nation. Biblically, the rainbow was a covenanted assurance given to Noah, by God, that the future world would be spared destruction by the means of a global flood.

"I have set my rainbow in the clouds, and it will be the sign of the covenant between me and the earth," the Lord declared. This is the covenant or a binding contract which God made, based on the relationship that existed between himself and Noah, who was a righteous man.

We in Anguilla have been traditionally known as a Christian nation. Well, not just as a Christian nation, but a *righteous* nation. It has been evident. There was much emphasis paid to religious norms and God's name was exalted all over the land. Churches were involved in spreading the gospel and people had a certain respect for the church and a fear for God. The churches were influential, and the nation was blessed. As the scripture declares in Psalm 33: 12, "Blessed is the nation whose God is the Lord."

Anguilla, as I knew it, had upheld the traditions and principles of godliness, modesty and morality. People of this nation honored God. And because the people honored Him, He blessed and favored them. For example, just about every young man was blessed with a portion of land, in years gone by. God had favored their forebears with their own land, and they were able to bequeath portions of property to their children. Then, with the land, every young man strove successfully to construct his own dwelling house. These were only some of the blessings and favor which God had covenanted with the people of this land.

God showed me where the residents of this island were desirous of being loyal to Him and his righteous precepts all throughout the ages of the islands civil history. Even when other surrounding islands had become infiltrated with vices and various kinds of open sin, Anguilla had been preserving its stance as a Christian nation.

The presence of the many rainbows, God said, had been a mark of His promise that should Anguilla retain its modesty and loyalty to Him, or even if the people who have slipped from his precepts returned to him, He will continue to be a guardian and a provider for the people. But he wanted me to show the people where they have erred. Here is what the Spirit wants Anguilla to know through these series of rainbows that have persistently flourished over this little island for three years from 2014 to 2016:

1. We are not sensitive to the Spirit of God, even though we base our spirituality as a God fearing and religious nation.
2. We are not sensitive to the Godly atmospheric protection that God has provided us with and do not recognize the evil circumstances that presents themselves on a daily basis.

3. We do not acknowledge or regard the persons who have contributed and are contributing significantly to our lives, spiritually.

4. We are not sensitive enough to God's creation, His mercy and His grace. We take things for granted and we are not grateful for God's favor and blessings. Therefore, there is no commitment to give Him glory. We find no time to praise him as we are to or worship Him for who He is.

5. We do not frequent God's house as we used to. Attending church is replaced with parting in secular activities of frolic and fun.

6. We fail to be thankful publicly for God's sovereignty. And then, we are simply not sensitive of His nearness to recognize His soon return.

Now, if we would consider our ways with regard to the preceding spiritual deficiencies; if we would repent and turn humbly to God, requesting Him to restore our relationship with Him, the "rainbow promise" is that He will forgive our sins and heal our land.

We must recognize in this season; it is critical for us as a nation to begin to give back to God glory and honor for His goodness towards us. And though the Bible declares in Isaiah 42:8, that God will not share His glory with man, He is saying, look at my creation; look at the signs and wonders I have created. How about the storms I have held back from your shores and disasters from your land over the years? Have you been noticing my handy works? Have you noticed the glory with which I have been blessing your nation?

Obviously, there is the need for us in Anguilla to praise the name of God and thank Him for His covenant promises to us. Sadly, instead of praising and thanking Him as we are to, many people have deliberately brought dishonor to His holy name. One of the greatest trends of iniquity is found in the disrespect for Christ's name and the profanity that erupts from the tongues of our people – especially our younger generation who are not sensitive to godly virtues.

Here what God says to Israel, and by extension to us, in Ezekiel 36:22: "I have concern for my holy name which the house of Israel had profaned among the nations…Thus saith the Lord God, I do not do this for your sake, but for MY holy name's sake, which you have profaned…"

What God is saying here is that if the people do not care to give glory to His name, then he will give glory to His *own* name. Just look at that! God is so amazing. He is so merciful. He does not treat us the way we deserve. It is written in Psalm 103:10, that "God has not dealt with us according to our sins, nor punished us according to our iniquities." All this gives interpretation to those symbolic rainbows. However, the people of Anguilla need to get back to the Lord and the precepts which our forefathers held dear and sacred.

The key denominator in the entire scenario of rainbows and their significance in the local Anguilla context is that the people who are called by God's name, the people who profess to know Christ as their Savior, needs to pray and praise God more.

God inhabits the praises of His people according to Psalms 22:3. Again, Psalms 19:1 tells of His supreme splendor as the heavens tell of the glory of God, and the firmament proclaims His great handiwork. Don't we see his awesome handiwork in the heavens as the Lord crafts his magnificent rainbows? How many of us mortals can do that? So, is He not worthy to be praised and glorified?

The symbolism of the rainbow to Noah was God's plan for showing mercy to those who were righteous in His sight. Wickedness had abounded in the world back then. But because Noah and his family were a righteous remnant, the scripture tells us: "Noah found grace in the eyes of the Lord," according to Genesis 6:8. And what did Noah do? Genesis 8:20 tells us that he built an altar of sacrifice unto the Lord and worshipped Him.

If God, who is supreme, can go out on a limb, so-to-speak, never to destroy this world with water ever again, how much more important it is for us to be committed to Him in gratitude, standing before Him with a sense of awe and honor as we gratefully worship His wonderful name.

God is faithful indeed. Just as he had been faithful to Noah, He has been faithful to us in Anguilla. Only thing, we are not to take his faithfulness and mercy for granted. We are to acknowledge Deuteronomy 7:9 which says: "Know therefore that the Lord your God, he is the faithful God, keeping his covenant and mercy for a thousand generations with those who love him and keep his commandments."

God's faithfulness reveals His plan for redemption, reconciliation, restoration, regeneration and reflection on His divine goodness. These virtues of the Lord's faithfulness encompass his glory.

God has a plan for making things complete and new, and whatever was destroyed He mercifully restores. This renewing attribute of God is seen in his restoration of the earth after the flood by which he had destroyed the Antediluvian World. The people of that world were wicked in God's sight. As the scripture says, "The Lord saw that the wickedness of man was great in the earth, and that the imagination of men's hearts was only evil continually."

Well, just as it was in the days of Noah, so it is today. And just as the Lord had provided an ark of escape for those who would heed Noah's extensive preaching, so he has provided a means of escape and redemption through giving to the world His son Jesus Christ who shed his blood for the remission of our sins. This is the perpetual covenant of blood.

When men everywhere accept the plan of salvation, they partake of the ultimate means of God's redemption. Lives that were broken and spirits that were dry and dead through sin would be made alive unto righteousness. Yes, God restores. Through His son Jesus Christ, He regenerates mankind and cause him to develop new growth – a new life in Christ. As a result, God receives the glory through this act of regeneration.

The rainbows that were so prevalent over Anguilla for those three years, 2014 thru 2016 marked the promise that if persons return to godly principles, then God world bless the land continually. Yes, Anguilla can remain blessed if we return to acknowledging God, despise the practices of unrighteous and uphold the precepts of righteousness.

In order to remain blessed, there is another condition we must adhere to. In these last days, it is easy for even the best of us to drift away from the precepts of right and indulge in the wrong. It is easy to displease God by our forbidden lifestyles. Therefore, it is essential that we travail in persistent prayers before Almighty God.

The days are evil. And Satan realizes that his time is short. He knows that the Lord will soon return and bring an end to all the misery and debacle which he has set out to imposes on God's people. That is why we must remain God-conscious and walk the straight and narrow as Jesus bids us to.

In illustrating the truth about walking the narrow road of righteousness, Jesus once said: "Wide is the gate and broad is the way that leads to destruction, and many are they that go into it; but narrow is the way that leads to life eternal and there are few that find it." Matthew 7:13-14. Yes, it is easy to drift into the wide way.

Satan is working more now overtime, upgrading his artillery against the children of God and oppressing them with various kinds of evil like never before. The devil is intercepting the will of God and making every effort to erase what God intends to be spirit-led and doable through our lives. This is why our faith and walk with Jesus Christ must be sealed tight so that no desire for us to do evil shall prevail over our will to do what is good and right.

Every day, followers of Christ are touched in some way, shape or form by Satan's evil intent. Satan buffets Christians regularly. He wants then to stop short of attaining the prize which God has promised them. He will cunningly rob their treasure of hope – the hope of their salvation – if they allow him to. The scripture says in John 10:10 "The devil comes to steal, kill and to destroy. This is his ultimate mission against all mankind on this earth, Christian or not.

However, it is rewarding and comforting to know that once we have surrendered to the Lord, we are His, and we can remain His by His power and by **our will**. We must be willing to stay under His seal with which he has sealed us until that day when Christ shall come. The scripture declares for us in 2 Timothy 2:19 "The foundation of God stands sure, and having this seal, the Lord knows those that are His..." However, the verse does not end there. The Apostle Paul, who wrote that assuring statement, goes further to give the follower of Christ a certain charge. He warns: ...And let everyone who names the name of Christ depart from iniquity." 2 Timothy 2:19. There is where **our will** comes into play. We must be **willing** to depart from iniquity and lay aside every weight, and the sin which so easily ensnares us.

In order to depart from iniquity, we must understand how import prayer is. Without it we will die. In fact, James Montgomery wrote an immortal hymn which says in part, "Prayer is the

Christian's vital breath, the Christian's vital air." Oh how we need to pray to steer clear of sinning. Jesus Himself, in teaching His disciples to pray, made a remarkable petition to God the Father in which he said: "...And lead us not into temptation, but deliver us from evil..." according to Matthew 6:13. What a caring Jesus. He knows that mankind would be most likely tempted to go in evil paths, and so he gave us that pattern of prayer as a mandate.

But you cannot just pray only in the mornings or in the night time. The Christian must have a certain appetite to prevail with fervent prayers. In 1 Thessalonians 5:17, we are encouraged to: "Pray without ceasing, for it is the will of God in Christ Jesus concerning you."

We are living in perilous times, according to 2 Timothy 3: 1-7. Here, the Apostle Paul lists a catalog of sins that will mark the perils that will come in the end time. As you read this list, bear in mind that only the power of prayer and faith in Jesus Christ can enable you to be immune in the evil day.

"In the last days," Paul says, "perilous times shall come, for men will be lovers of themselves; lovers of money, boasters, proud, blasphemers, disobedient to parents, unthankful, unholy, unloving, unforgiving, slanders, without self-control, brutal, despisers of good, led away with various lusts, always learning and never coming to the knowledge of truth, headstrong, haughty, lovers of pleasure rather than lovers of God.

The signs of these perilous times are also clear in Matthew 24: 4-8. Here, Jesus encourages us to take heed that no one deceives us. He said: "Many will come in my name, saying I am the Christ and will deceive many. False prophets will rise up and deceive many. You will hear of wars and rumors of wars; nation will arise against nation; and kingdom will rise against kingdom. There will be famines, pestilences, and earthquakes in various places; lawlessness will abound and the love of many will grow cold. All these are the beginning of sorrows that must come to pass before the end come."

As followers of Christ and believers in his doctrines, we must pay attention to how Jesus closes off this prophecy to his disciples in Matthew 24:9. He warns: "You will be delivered up to tribulation and will be killed, and you will be hated by all nations for my sake." But, we are encouraged to endure to the end, for only those who endure to the end shall be saved. May it be our will, our aim and our determination to endure to the end, for it will be worth it all when we see Christ.

Chapter 21:

"The Meaning of the Rainbow"

The significance of the rainbow has been a prominent feature in human history since God made his covenant with Noah. Ever since then, it has been a symbol of hope to cultures across the globe.

Here is what God's declaration was to Noah: "I set my rainbow in the cloud, and it shall be for a token of a covenant between me and the earth. It shall come to pass, when I bring a cloud over the earth, that the rainbow shall be seen in the cloud. I will remember my covenant, which is between me and you, and every living creature of all flesh and the waters shall no longer become a flood to destroy all flesh." Genesis 9:12-15.

Interestingly, the rainbow was initially mentioned in the first book of the Bible, Genesis, and it was last alluded to in the last book of the Bible, Revelation. A reference to a rainbow is also found in the first chapter of the book of Ezekiel. In the Genesis account, a rainbow appeared just after the great worldwide flood which was God's method of removing or purging sin and evil-minded humanity from the earth.

That rainbow symbolized God's mercy and His Covenant with Noah, who represents mankind. The statement of its symbolism is that the world will never again be destroyed by floods of water. That was the first meaning of the rainbow – a symbol of God's gracious promise.

The book of Ezekiel records that in Ezekiel's, his first vision from God, known as the "Wheel in the Middle of a Wheel" vision, the prophet compared the Glory of God, as he saw it, with a rainbow.

Here is Ezekiel's account. "Above the firmament over their heads was the likeness of a throne, in the appearance of a sapphire stone, and upon the likeness of the throne was the likeness as the appearance of a man high above upon it.

"Also, from the appearance of his waist upward, I saw, as it were, the color of amber, as the appearance of fire all around within it; and from the appearance of his loins upward, and from the appearance of his loins, even downward, I saw, as it were, the appearance of fire, and it had brightness around about it. As the appearance of the rainbow that is in the cloud on a rainy day, so was the appearance of the brightness all around it. *This was the appearance of the likeness of the*

glory of the Lord. And when I saw it, I fell upon my face, and I heard a voice of one that spoke." Ezekiel 1:26-28. This was the second meaning of the rainbow – a representation of the glory of the Lord.

Rainbows appear again in the prophetic book of Revelation, which foretells the end of man's rule on the earth and the coming of Jesus to set up His Kingdom. As it was in Ezekiel, the first mention of a rainbow in Revelation appears when the Apostle John used it to ***describe the glory and power of God on His throne.***

John in Revelation says: "After this I looked, and behold a door was opened in heaven and the first voice which I heard was, as it were, of a trumpet talking with me, which said, come up hither and I will show thee things which must be hereafter. And immediately, I was in the spirit and behold a throne was set in heaven, and one sat on the throne. He that sat on the throne was to look upon like Jasper and a Sardine stone and there was a rainbow round about the throne, like unto an Emerald." Revelation 4:1-3. ***Here again we see that John the Revelator sees, as rainbows, the splendor of God's glory as he is sitting on His throne.***

The second mention of a rainbow in Revelation is recorded when John describes the look of a mighty angel. It says, "And I saw another mighty angel come down from heaven clothed with a cloud and a rainbow was upon his head and his face, as it were, was like the sun, and his feet as pillars of fire," Revelation 10:1. ***Here, once again, it is obvious that the rainbow symbolizes glory.*** It is no so much the glory of God in this instance, but the glory which he has attributed to the angel with a rainbow upon his head.

So what about the colors in the rainbow? What do they symbolize? The root meaning of the colors of the rainbow in scripture are the basis for recognizing the beauty of God's grace. Both the prophet Ezekiel and John the Revelator, compare the rainbow colors to the glory of God. Each of the original eight rainbow colors represents an idea: pink for sexuality; red for life; orange for healing; yellow for the sun; green for nature; blue for art, indigo for harmony; and violet for spirit.

The sequence of colors in the rainbow matches seven days of re-creation, and everything in creation conforms to the Holiness or Sanctification of God. The rainbow is produced by the sanctification of white light, and all of creation conforms to the colors of the rainbow.

Where there is light, there is God, but the true interpretation of that light is only possible by means of faith. Every scene of life has meaning in the fulfillment of the plan of God and in the life of the believer.

The rainbow colors are always consistent with definition from the Word of God. This is the plan of God in the life of the believer. God has laid out your life's plan in His Word from Genesis to Revelation and from one end of the Rainbow to the other.

If you have not yet received the free gift of salvation which would enable you to be glorified with Christ in His glorious Kingdom when he returns, then I encourage you to put your trust in Him today, for His return is not too far away. He died on the cross so that we could have the free gift of eternal life. And He is worth more than a "Pot of Gold" at the end of any rainbow.

My Daily Experience of Living in the Sphere of the Rainbow

I am one who believes with childlike faith in the promises of God, my Father. I believe that when he makes *a promise* or *a covenant* as He had made with His servants of old, that covenant is sealed, and as we sometimes say his promises are "yeah and Amen". And yes, I believe that God speaks His promises to us through signs and wonders, as He has spoken his promises to me.

In 2020, I purchased some windows for my dwelling studio that was under construction at the time. When I furnished the extension and started occupying it, I began noticing rainbow patterns throughout the floor and on objects inside in every room that was protected by these windows.

My common sense told me that it is probably the prisms rays of sunlight that is formed on the windows, are causing these rainbow reflections to appear. I guess persons who purchased the same windows experience the same appearances. In the past and especially after we were experiencing rainbows phenomena in 2014, every time I wake up in the mornings, the first thing I used to do is to look outside in the sky for a rainbow. Now, though,

I have my own replicas of rainbows all over the interior of my house, and I constantly bask, consciously, in the promises of God. If that is not a blessing, then you tell me what is.

However, I felt like God intended for me to live in the experience though not actual rainbows from creation, these mechanical prisms from the windows are just as amazing to watch. I could have purchased some other choice windows, but my mind was set to purchase these and I had no idea what the makeup of these windows were, and although I was told of cheaper options, somehow, I was determined to purchase the ones I was led by the spirit to purchase and now, I am experiencing rainbows in my house all day as long as the sun is shining. Blessings, upon blessings can't done!

Do you call that coincidence? In 2012, God showed me a rainbow in a vision. I was keen and inspired to display the colors of the rainbow on a table in a corner of our church, the No Walls Church of Hope Ministry. Two years later, in 2014, the prophecy regarding the rainbow was fulfilled, as rainbows were seen all across the island of Anguilla for a period, {apart from the rarely seen rainbows} for about two years and months from November, 2014 into 2016. I was inspired by the Holy Spirit in the later part of November 2014, to write about the rainbow, God's Covenant with Anguilla.

Again, do you call this a coincidence? No! I say the Holy Spirit inspired me to call this supernatural phenomenal into being, according to Romans 4:16-17. After I received the vision, I begin to envision seeing a rainbow. Almost every day, I would be looking up into the skies with anticipation and expectation to see a rainbow. And then, I believed, God created a bit of earthly phenomenal manifesting grace for me to experience and to enjoy a shadowy replica of rainbows.

These rainbows are evident all day in doors as long as the sun is shining. They can be seen on the living room chairs, in the bathroom, on the bed and my grandson, Jai would just lie there, saying he is lying down on a rainbow or he would say he's catching a rainbow on the kitchen counter and in the kitchen sink. They are everywhere in the house and sometimes till late in the evening, just like they were occurring in real time across Anguilla.

For me, it is so amazing, not only to be given the vision of the rainbow, but to write about the rainbow and see the prophecy be fulfilled and now, to be living and basking in a replica fashion of rainbows on a daily basis, as long as the sun shines? Man, this is some wonder God has performed, and I am enjoying it every day. Because of this, I am reminded and I am grateful for His provision and greatness on a daily basis. It is hard for me to go through the day without give Him ardent worship. And it is also no coincidence that my ministry's logo depicts also the colors of the rainbow. Only God could have caused this amazement and phenomenal experience. Blessed be His Holy name!

Chapter 22:

"Working For a Crown That Fades Not Away"

It was with much intent that the title of this book was crafted. "The Life-Testimony and Work of God's Servant" reflects the service that I have rendered to God who has been the strength of my life throughout my years on this earth.

From my youthful days of accepting Christ as my Savior and Shepherd, I have risen through the ranks of church service. I have had visions that caused me to work for the Lord, while others receive the benefits of healing, deliverance and the breaking of oppressive chains. My work and mission have been, and continue to be, all to the glory of God.

It is essential to understand that I am not working in God's vineyard for myself. "It is not about me", as the saying goes. And I would like to testify that every victory and every achievement in my life and work, spiritually and otherwise, go toward the glory and honor of God Almighty.

I, like all others ministers who are called to work for God, I am responsible to serve him as a humble servant. He is my Lord whom I glorify through the way I live and through the service that I give. It continues to be my utmost interest and my desire to be used as an effective and efficient instrument in His Kingdom for which Christ prayed to come to this earth. Yes, His Kingdom has come. It is in the "here and now", and it is a wonderful privilege for me to be a part of the great work that fulfills the mission of the Kingdom of God.

As a servant of Christ, I wish to draw a specific analogy to the spirit of a sheep. I am His sheep – humble, pliable and flexible, led by His nail scarred hands. His wishes are my commands and, as such, I am committed to follow where my gentle Shepherd leads me. I know that at the end of this journey, I shall receive a glorious crown for the service I have rendered. As the old song says, "I am working for a crown". However, that crown is not my only focus. It is not my greatest interest. The work that I do for the Master keeps me involved in His field of service while I wait for that crowning day. You see, the Apostle Peter once told us in 1 Peter 5:4, "When the Chief Shepherd appears, you will receive the crown of glory that does not fade away." Yes, one day Christ, the Chief Shepherd, Jesus Himself, will appear. And as the scriptures declare in 2 Timothy 4:8, "Henceforth there is laid up for me a crown of righteousness which the Lord, the righteous judge shall give me at that day."

I realize that crown of glory, also called a crown of righteousness, will be my ultimate rich reward. All of us love to receive rewards for work we do down here. Trophies adorn our living rooms and offices; certificates and plaques decorate our walls as testaments of our great achievements. They serve as significant hallmarks for what we have accomplished. But they will ultimately tarnish and fade away, like everything else that is material.

The faithful Apostle Peter was careful to remind us, though, that the glorious crown which will be given by the hand of our Chief Shepherd will be one that fades not away – a perpetual, eternal, everlasting crown of glory.

I continue to carry on His work as the Lord gives me the wherewithal to labor for Him. It is my intent to occupy myself in this Ministry to bless and benefit others, while I honor and glorify Christ. And so, I am busying myself in His employ. Being with Jesus my Savior, when He appears, that will be my most treasured reward.

I am reminded of His loyal promise to us just before He left this dreary earth, according to John 14:2-3. He faithfully promised: "I go to prepare a place for you, and if I go to prepare a place for you, I will come again and receive you unto myself, so that where I am, there you may be also." Yes, I want to be with Jesus, where He is. I am not earthbound. This world is not my home. To be with Him, the one whom I love and the one who loves me enough to sacrifice His life for my redemption, it is **my greatest joy ever, that one day; I will live and reign with Him eternally.**

Ultimately, even more important than attaining that crown which fades not away, I just want to be with Jesus at "the end of the day". I want to be present with Him who died for me – the one who was gracious enough to provide ransom for this world with His own blood; the one who was wounded for our transgressions and bruised for our iniquities... and by whose stripes we are healed.

And oh! How rewarding Heaven will be—it is not just to wear a crown of Glory; not just to walk those streets of gold; but just because Jesus will be there.

In fact, Heaven is a place of perfect peace and rest. According to Revelation 21:4-5, which says," That God, Himself, will wipe away every tear from our eyes. There shall be no more death, no sorrow, no crying. There will be no more pain, for the former things have passed away. And verse 5 continues to say, then He who sat on the throne said, "Behold I make all things new." And He said to me, "Write, for these words are true and faithful.

And as Donnie MacClurkins rightfully sings, "As Long As You Are There". Let us depth the heavenly joy that awaits us through these immortal words:

As Long As You Are There

If there were no gates of pearl
If there were no streets of gold
If there was no other world oh ooo uh
In a land where we won't grow old uh huh

I'm not thinking about those sites, no ooh
Won't be there to enjoy the view, no ooh
I think heaven will be alright
Just as long as you are there
As long as there is you

If I never hear an Angel sings
In a far off holy land
If I never hear a joy bell ring
Sing a chorus in a Christian band

I'm not thinking about those sites
Won't be there to enjoy the view

I think heaven will be alright
Just as long as you are there
As long as there is you

If I were to say why I wrote this book, the reason would be perfectly wrapped up in seven immortal words: "to tell of the goodness of God".

I am sure that I speak for true Christians everywhere when I say that God has been good to us. If you are a genuine Christian, it is no doubt that you, too, can rightfully attest to the fact that "God is good". By the way, he is not just "good", but I am sure you would agree that He is "great". His greatness and goodness are evident throughout the entire earth – throughout the farthest reaches of His great universe.

This book relates how the hand of God has rested upon my life from the moment that I yielded to His son, Jesus, who once said: *"Come unto me. All ye who are weary and heavy laden and I will give you rest."*

This book describes the circumstances under which I yielded my life to Christ. It tells how I developed in the Lord from the youthful stage of a child, coming up in the ranks of church life. It relates how great an impact my hometown church has had upon my upbringing through the quality mentorship of my Pastors and Elders.

This book, ***The Life-Testimony and Work of God's Servant***, reflects an account of my spiritual development and devotion to the Lord, who called me to live a life of light and purpose before Him. Very importantly, it shows how God uses a life that is surrendered to His divine will in order reach out to others who are in need of healing, restoration and His divine protection.

I have prayed that persons reading my book that the Holy Spirit will come upon you to give you a sense of connection with Him, to help to align yourself with His truth and to cause a renewal of spirit to serve God and to find your purpose in Him.

I also pray that your understanding be open up to healing and supernatural miracles in your own life and that the Spirit of God will come upon you as you are inspired by the testimonies shared. So, please savior the reading as the Holy Spirit directs your thoughts and life.

Chapter 23:

"A Prayer Warrior - A Word From Patison"

Greetings and blessings to you, dear reader. I'm Patison, Patricia's second son. I hope you've been blessed so far from the pages you've read. If you'd bear with me a bit longer, I'd like to give a little testimony relating to the love of a mother.

You see, my Mom (my Queen) asked me to give her a hand with the final preparations of this project, by formatting and getting the publishing done. I actually gave her a timeline of about two weeks to get it done. I guess I owe you an apology for the unforeseen delay in that case, as life threw some trials and tribulations my way that meant this dream of hers had to be paused a while longer.

It was just about the end of the second week when Mom called (around 10pm UK time, June 5th 2023) to check on the progress and give instructions of few amendments to make. I was at a restaurant having dinner. I answered the phone, softly. Almost whispering, you know...as you do when you don't want to disturb the company you're with. In honesty, I wasn't feeling too well and would have rather been at home at that particular moment. The call was a short one, less than a minute, and we agreed to catch up the next day.

Well...Mom being Mom, must have sensed something in my voice that didn't sit right in her spirit. Something troubling enough to cause her to not sleep that night until she offered up a prayer of protection for me. From what I can put together, it was in the early morning hours of June 6th, 2023 that she was in prayer...while I was calling for an ambulance.

Around 2.30am a pain like nothing I've experienced before suddenly thumped in my head. The pain spread down my neck and across my shoulders in steady, heavy waves. It hurt to talk, to open my eyes, even to breathe. Eventually, I made it to the hospital, where after sometime, a CT scan showed that I had an intracranial bleed. Basically, an aneurysm in my brain was on the brink of rupturing, which could have caused me life changing damages...or death.

At 5.13am Mom sent me a WhatsApp message saying "...I've decided to leave it. Forget about it". Now, I later found out that she'd sent that message after spending some time praying for me feeling that I was already heavily stressed and she didn't want to add to it. Bless her. The day after my surgery, doctors admitted that my issue was most likely heavily caused by high levels of stress. What can I say? Life.

Now, ever since I was a young, teen Christian, I've sometimes wondered why God would allow certain things to happen to his people. We've all found ourselves in these thoughts at one point or another, no? Why would he allow a hurricane to destroy an entire island, where his beloved lived? Why would he allow his beloved to suffer terrible accidents? Why would he allow me to have a brain bleed that could have killed me?

But then...I remember, He will never put more on me than I can bear. Amen? And the reason I can bear such an experience and be alive today is because I have the love of a discerning mother who bears may trials with me (silently and from a distance even) and upholds me in prayer. And so do you! It may not be a mother, but a brother or sister. A friend, or a stranger who feels you're inner most spiritual needs and makes the decision to go before the Lord in prayer on your behalf. Give thanks for the prayer warriors out there.

I give thanks for the love of my prayer warrior. My Queen.

Dedication:

This Book is dedicated to my Mom: Hellen Alicia Mason (deceased).

To my three sons: Patmore, Patison and Patville.

My four grandsons: Jai, Kaedyn, Dylan and Malachi.

You are my gifts from God. I pray that your lives will have legacies laid up only to the Most High, God, but that you will also impact humanity in a meaningful and positive ways.

You have been a great source of love and encouragement. You have honored me not only as your Mother, but an example, and as a Queen.

From a Mother's heart, you are my delight, you are my inspiration, and totally, you are my pillars of strength. I declare that you shall walk in the fullness of your purpose and destiny.

Acknowledgement:

I give ardent thanks: Firstly, to Almighty God for His calling upon my life and allowing me His grace and mercy, setting me apart to work in His Kingdom.

To the Editor: James Harrigan, for his time and effort with his unique touch of editorial finesse.

To my sons, Patison and Patville who are duly gifted with abilities to create and design and Patmore assisted with his computer skills in the production of:

The Life-Testimony and Work of a Servant of God.

My Personal Condensed Book Resume:

Education:

Johnson & Wales University – Providence, Rhode Island, USA

Barton Medical School – Scranton, PA, USA

Data Institution, Waterbury, CT, USA

American Hotel & Lodging Association, (AH&LA), USA, Hospitality Supervisor/Manager-Program

Job Experiences:

Chase Manhattan Bank, St. Marten, NA (Bank's Loan Originator/Secretary/Performance-Award) – St. Maarten, NA

Government Executive/Administrative Assistant – Anguilla, BWI

Hospitality Supervisor/Manager and Villas Manager – Anguilla, BWI

Dick International, Office Administrator – Anguilla, BWI

Tandem, Office Manager – Anguilla, BWI

Small Business Program – Anguilla, BWI

Professional Secretary Recognition –Anguilla, BWI

E-mail: pharrigan428@gmail.com

Printed in Great Britain
by Amazon